HELLO
EVERYBODY,
This is Cawood Ledford

HELLO EVERYBODY,
This is Cawood Ledford

*The story of a Kentucky legend,
as told to Billy Reed*

Host Creative Communications
Lexington, Kentucky

Copyright ® 1992 by Host Creative Communications

All rights reserved. No part of this publication may be reproduced without the permission of the publisher.

"Hello Everybody, This is Cawood Ledford" is published and printed by Host Creative Communications, 904 North Broadway, Lexington, Kentucky 40505, (606) 252-6681.

Edited by Ed Kromer and Tom Wallace
Cover design and layout by Michaela Duzyk
Photo album design by Nanci Lamar
Distributed by Kevin Halstead and Julie Sherrard

Photography by David Coyle, Bill Luster. Some photos were provided by the University of Kentucky Sports Communications office and Cawood Ledford's personal collection.

ISBN: 1-879688-17-4

Acknowledgements

Doing a book of any sort is a difficult undertaking. It's even more difficult when the book is an autobiography, where you're constantly sifting through the memory bank in hopes of finding and dusting off a lot of old and forgotten memories. To do that, and then to get it all down on paper in an interesting way, requires the gigantic efforts of many people, some of whom helped without even knowing it.

However, there are several people I would like to acknowledge, because without them this project couldn't have become a reality.

First, I would like to thank Billy Reed, an outstanding writer who worked diligently with me to bring this book into print. I'd also like to thank Billy for his patience. Goodness knows, I'm sure I tried his patience on more than one occasion.

A big thanks goes to Tom Wallace, the editor of my newspaper, *Cawood on Kentucky,* for his many contributions. Along with giving me many great suggestions, Tom also pored through the manuscript to make sure it was accurate.

My appreciation to Kim Ramsay in my office for mothering this book from start to finish. She spent many hours on this project.

I must give a big thanks to the people at Host Creative Communications Publishing for their unfailing cooperation, with a special nod to Rick Ford, J.D. Rutledge, Ed Kromer,

Nanci Lamar and Kevin Halstead.

Doing this book reminded me once again just how fortunate I've been to work with so many great people through the years, like the people at WHLN in Harlan who gave me my start, and the staffs at WLEX in Lexington and WHAS in Louisville. Also, thanks to G.H. Johnston Co., Host Creative Communications and the Kentucky Network, all of whom have owned the UK broadcasting rights at one time during my career. They've all been a pleasure to work with.

I'd like to give a special mention to Ralph Gabbard and his staff at WKYT-TV in Lexington. They've been colleagues and great friends for many years.

That holds true for all those people who have worked with me through the years on the UK broadcasts. I'd especially like to thank my broadcasting family over the past several years — Ralph Hacker, Tom Devine, Dave Baker and Dick Gabriel.

I'm extremely grateful and indebted to Jim Host, the CEO of Host Creative Communications, who has been my business partner for the past 13 years and a dear friend for more than 25 years.

And one of the biggest thanks is saved for all the coaches, players and administrators at UK throughout my 39-year association with that wonderful university. Their cooperation and friendship have made my job a true joy.

And, finally, I would like to thank my wife Frances, who stood with me every step of the way. She was a wonderful source of information, and she continually offered ways to make this a more worthy book. She is truly my better half.

Contents

To Frances,
The greatest Lady
on the face of the earth

Foreword

By Billy Reed

W hen Cawood Ledford asked me to work on this book with him, my first reaction was to be thrilled and flattered. Of all the people I've been around in my 33 years as a sportswriter with *Sports Illustrated*, the *Lexington Herald-Leader* and *The Courier-Journal*, I can't think of anybody whom I like or respect more than the "Voice of the Wildcats."

I literally grew up with Cawood because his first season of calling UK games, 1953-54, also was the first winter I remember following the Wildcats. My favorite player was Cliff Hagan, because he was so darned handsome and so darned good. I thought my heart would break that season when I got up the nerve to ask Cliff to autograph my program. He agreed, but just as he was beginning to sign his name, the pencil point broke. I'm sure there's a moral there somewhere, but I can't figure out what it is.

When I finally met Cawood as a young sportswriter in the 1960s, I felt we had known each other for years. After all, he had come into my home, through the radio, so many times that he was sort of like family. I know a lot of people around Kentucky understand exactly what I'm talking about. How many cold winter nights have we all spent hunkered up next to the radio, listening to Cawood describe the Cats' fate in some faraway place?

I've lived in Kentucky my whole life, except for three-and-a-half years from 1968 through 1972 when I went to New York to work for *Sports Illustrated*. The times when I'd get the most homesick were when I went to the Kentucky Derby and heard them play "My Old Kentucky Home," and on nights when UK would be playing a big game in Memorial Coliseum. Several times I remember driving around Long Island, trying to find a spot where I could get the 50,000-watt signal of WHAS. The sound of Cawood's call comforted me, but it also created a yearning. Listening to him, I could close my eyes and envision those sweet, familiar scenes: Coach Rupp up stomping his foot, the band playing the fight song, the guys in the white uniforms hustling up and down the polished hardwood, the squeaks of their sneakers lost in the bedlam.

When I first met Cawood, I suppose I was a little apprehensive, maybe even intimidated. He always seemed so urbane and sophisticated with his tailored suits, his cigarettes and coffee, his jaunty smile. Yet it didn't take me long to discover that he was as regular a guy as you'll ever find. I've heard it said that the definition of a gentleman is one who is at home in any company. Well, that's Cawood. He's the same whether he's talking to a blueblood Bluegrass horse breeder from Central Kentucky or a tobacco-stained coal miner from his native Eastern Kentucky. He just likes people, that's all, and he's so down to earth that he makes everyone, and anyone, feel comfortable.

Comfortable. That's the operative word with Cawood. The great turf writer Joe Palmer once likened a visit to Keeneland to an evening spent with slippers and brandy before the fire. So it is with Cawood. He's been there for us for so long, in the good years and bad, helping us momentarily forget our troubles, that we're going to miss him terribly. So long as Cawood was around, we had an anchor, a friend, a link to the past. There's something about radio, perhaps, that creates a closeness, a bond, that you just don't get from TV. Maybe because radio forces us to use our imaginations, its announcers — the good ones, at least — become dream weavers who create tapestries for our minds. This is a craft, an art, and nobody has ever done it better than Cawood.

Although writing requires a different set of tools than announcing, I've noticed that the best people in both fields — at least, the ones I've come to admire — share certain traits. A certain amount of talent is involved, of course, but there's also a willingness to work hard, to do the job right no matter what it takes, and a fierce pride in yourself. And just as coaches preach incessantly about fundamentals and execution, so are the most successful journalists the ones who do their homework, who prepare themselves the best and who then translate that preparation into a piece of work that merits the attention, and respect, of the public. The thing I've always liked about Cawood is that he understands that substance is just as important as style. So instead of getting hung up on gimmicks or tomfoolery, Cawood just gives you a steady diet of solid, accurate, colorful reporting — the essence of journalism, whatever the medium.

Over the years, Cawood has received enough honors and awards to fill a small museum. He's the only person to be inducted into both the Kentucky Journalism Hall of Fame and the Kentucky Athletic Hall of Fame. He has been named Kentucky's Sportscaster of the Year more than 20 times by the National Sportscasters and Sports Writers Association. I know he's especially fond of his Eclipse Awards, given for meritorious reporting of thoroughbred racing, because Cawood has a special place in his heart for the racing game, especially the Kentucky Derby.

Ordinarily, when a guy receives so many honors, a certain amount of jealousy will rear its ugly head among his peers. But not with Cawood. I've never heard anybody begrudge him a single honor because of the kind of professional he always has been. Even in his later years, when it would have been easy to coast and trade on his reputation, Cawood only seemed to work harder, always setting the example for the rest of us.

A few years ago, my wife Donna and I had dinner with Cawood and his bride Frances. The women hit it off famously, which pleased both Cawood and me. Since then, we've spent so many pleasant evenings together that the only good thing about Cawood retiring, from my standpoint, is that maybe now we'll be able to see even more of each other. I think it'll be fun to go to games, or the races, and just enjoy them, like everyone else, without having to worry about the things that trouble all of us in this crazy business: Did I do a good job? Did I miss anything? Did I make any mistakes? Was I fair? What am I going to do tomorrow?

In closing, let me say that working with Cawood on this book has been even more enjoyable and delightful than I imagined it would be. For me, it was fun to hear new stories, told as only Cawood can tell them, and relive old ones. I can't tell you how many times our taping would be interrupted because both of us would crack up laughing over something Coach Rupp had said, once upon a time, or some other funny nugget that one of us would pull from our memories. I'll always be honored that Cawood asked me to help and I'll always cherish the experience.

I only hope our finished product gives each of you a small fraction of the pleasure you've gotten all these years from the broadcasts of this special gentleman, this consummate professional, this beloved old friend.

Billy Reed
Louisville, Ky.
April 1, 1992

Chapter 1

Hello Everybody, This is Cawood Ledford

*I*t all started with a phone call from Charlie Ward.

Charlie was the basketball coach at Hall High School in Harlan County when I was also a member of the faculty there. However, at the end of the 1951 basketball season, Charlie left coaching to take a job selling commercials and doing sports for radio station WHLN in Harlan. The following summer, Charlie called to suggest that we meet for coffee. He told me he liked his job at the radio station, but that he couldn't get coaching out of his blood. He wanted to get back into the coaching business, which meant he needed to make his availability known in order to get one of the positions that might open up. Charlie then informed me that he was going to resign from the station and that he wanted to recommend me for the job.

That's how it all started, and that was the luckiest thing that ever happened to me.

Since I announced my retirement, I've had a lot of people ask me why I'm doing it now. I'm 66, not exactly ancient, and my health is still good. And although I might be fooling myself, I don't think I've slipped any. I try to really listen to the tapes of the games and to criticize myself. I also ask my wife, Frances, to give me her opinion. She tells me I sound as good as ever, but, then, I'm not sure she would ever say anything else.

The thing is, I just didn't want somebody to call me up someday and say, "It's time for you to go and we're going to get somebody else." That's what the Detroit Tigers did to Ernie Harwell, and look how sad that was for everybody. CBS did the same thing to Jack Buck, one of the finest sports announcers in America. So this way I was able to name the time without having somebody else do it for me. Besides, it gave everybody a year to decide what they wanted to do, and the University of Kentucky deserved that, as great as those people have been to me all this time.

Once I made the decision, I felt a great sense of relief. Then the mail started coming in and I must admit I was overwhelmed. Until then, I thought the highest honor I had ever received — even more than being inducted into the Kentucky Athletic Hall of Fame and the Kentucky Journalism Hall of Fame — was when the University of Kentucky retired a jersey in my honor. I was completely surprised, had no idea they were going to do anything like that, because they had never done it for anybody except a player or a coach. However, I think all the mail I got, and am still getting, even topped that. I'm talking about long, personal letters about what listening to me and the Wildcats has meant over the years. It's been extremely touching and rewarding, I can tell you that.

I think one of the big things that has really helped me is

the fact that I was born and raised in a little town up in the mountains of Eastern Kentucky. Because of that, I think UK fans always accepted me a little more than if I'd been from somewhere else. My home is Cawood, which was named after my mother's family. I was the oldest of three children and was the worst athlete of the bunch. My sister, Eloise, was a gifted pianist and a good tennis player. My brother, Jim, was a good high school football and baseball player. My father, James Washington "Wash" Ledford, had been a pretty good baseball player in his younger days on some of the teams sponsored by the coal companies. He knew Earle Combs, who went on to become the center fielder next to Babe Ruth on those great New York Yankee teams of the 1920s. Still, the real sports fan in the family was my mother, Sudie. She listened to all the sports events, but the one I think she loved most was the Kentucky Derby. She just loved horses. Much later in her life, I'd bring her to Keeneland where she and Frances would split $2 bets.

My mother had been a school teacher when she and my father married. Since I was the oldest, she spent a lot of time reading to me and teaching me. She said I could recite nursery rhymes by the time I was 18 months old. Her father told her that anyone who could talk as early and as well as I did would become either a lawyer or a preacher. He didn't know about broadcasting back then or he probably would have included that profession as well.

My mother wanted me to be a pharmacist, I guess

because two of her brothers were doctors. One of them — the father of my cousin Dave Cawood, who's now an executive with the NCAA — wanted me to be a doctor and encouraged me to go into medicine. It just never had any appeal to me. But really, all my mom ever told me was that she wanted me to try to be the best at whatever I did. I always remembered that.

Anyway, as an athlete I was just what Coach Adolph Rupp would have called "one of the turds." I suppose that's how a lot of sports announcers and writers end up doing what they do. We love sports, but the only way we can participate is to talk about it or write about it. So at Hall High School and later on at Centre College, I wrote for the school paper.

I really didn't get hooked on Kentucky basketball until I was at Centre. I had some friends from Harlan who went to UK, including Wah Wah Jones, who was a great all-sports star for the Wildcats in the late 1940s. So a bunch of us would go from Danville over to Lexington to watch UK play in old Alumni Gym. Those, of course, were the days of the "Fabulous Five." You want to talk about great basketball teams, that's where you begin. I still think it was the best team the university has ever had — Ralph Beard, Alex Groza, Cliff Barker, Kenny Rollins and, of course, Wah Wah. They were really something.

When I graduated from Centre in 1949, being a sports announcer was the farthest thing from my mind. I went back home and took a job with Modern Bakery in Harlan. It was owned by Elmer Hall, one of the finest gentlemen I've ever known. I worked in the office, but after a couple of years, I knew it wasn't the kind of work that I was cut out for. I wasn't sure what I wanted to do. One day the county superintendent of schools, James A. Cawood — who also happened to be my first cousin — called me and told me he needed a teacher at Hall High. I told him that I really wasn't qualified to be a teacher since my degree was in business administration and that I didn't have any education courses. He said, "Well you've got a degree and you're the best I can do on short notice." I thought, what the hell, I'll give it a shot.

I had been taught English at Hall by Mildred Rowland and, fortunately, Mrs. Rowland was the school principal when I went there to teach. She was an excellent administrator and an indispensable help to me when I ran into problems with teaching English in the classroom. I was flattered at the end of the school year when Mrs. Rowland asked me to take some education courses during the summer and return to Hall that fall. I really loved teaching, but I couldn't bear the thought of going back to school.

While at Hall High, Charlie Ward asked if I would help with the basketball team that semester. I did, and that led to us becoming good friends. I enjoyed working with the team so much that semester that I gave some thought to becoming a coach. But I realized I was probably not the next Adolph

Rupp and that I needed to find a different kind of work.

After the phone call from Charlie that summer, he made an appointment for me to meet with the owners of WHLN, Dick Helm and Francke Fox. It was the first time in my life I had ever been inside a radio station. The interview went well, and Dick asked me if I would come back to the station that night and make an audition tape. I remember that Murray Worner was on the board that night and he had pulled some news copy off The Associated Press machine. He also included a couple of commercials for me to record. He asked me if I'd like to listen to the tape. I said yes. That's when I heard, for the first time, my own voice. It was terrible. Dick and Francke apparently didn't agree. I got a call in a day or two from Dick. He offered me the job for $45 a week. I jumped at it.

The first sport I did was baseball — the Harlan Smokies Class D team in the old Mountain States League. I also did high school football and basketball. Hall, Harlan, Loyall, Evarts, Lynch, Cumberland, Benham — I did 'em all, sometimes three games a weekend. That was in '51.

Somebody once said that to steal from one person is plagiarism, but to steal from many is research. If that's true, I was one of the great researchers, because I admired a lot of the big-name announcers at the time, and I stole from every one of them. Red Barber, Bill Stern, Ted Husing, Clem McCarthy, Bryan Field and a fellow I always liked a lot, Al Helfer, on the baseball Game of the Day. I was a great admirer of Ed Murrow; I really tried to study his style. I also got tremendous help and encouragement from two of my colleagues at WHLN, Jay Barlow and Jim Morgan.

In the winter of 1953, I returned to the radio station from doing a Harlan basketball game. The announcer working the night shift told me that I had a call from Bob Cox at the Lewallen Hotel and that Bob had asked that I give him a call. Bob told me he really liked my work and was wondering if I'd be interested in working in Lexington. Well, that sounded like CBS to me. I met Bob the next morning at the Court Cafe. It turned out that he was an executive with the Schine theaters, and he also kept stats for Claude Sullivan, who was then doing the UK games for WVLK and the Standard Oil Network. Bob told me there was about to be a turnover at WLEX. "If you're interested," he said, "I'll see what I can do for you."

Well, that was February and I didn't get a call until August. Bob called to say the job had finally opened up at WLEX and that he had scheduled me an appointment. I went to Lexington for the interview and was hired on the spot. I had doubled my salary in two years at WHLN to $90 a week and that was exactly what I was offered by WLEX. When you consider that I would be paying to rent a room and buying my own meals, it actually was a losing proposition. But I didn't care. Here I was, just four years out of college, and I felt like I was in the big time.

Chapter 2

The Bear And The Baron

*M*y first fall covering UK games also was Bear Bryant's last season as the Wildcat football coach. I went to practice every day that year and I couldn't get over how brutal it was. When I mentioned that to one of the players, he said, "This is nothing to the way it used to be."

I guess Bryant really was a bear in his first few years at UK. I remember there was just this aura around him. He commanded so much respect. That team lost its first two games, but then Bryant put Bob Hardy at quarterback and they didn't lose again. They finished 7-2-1 by beating Tennessee in the last game, something Bryant hadn't been able to do with his teams that went to the big bowls. I was as surprised as anybody after the season when Bryant announced that he was leaving Lexington to go to Texas A&M, of all places.

The first time I met Bryant, he told me how good he thought Claude Sullivan and J.B. Faulconer were. I was more familiar with J.B. because his radio network, the Ashland Oil Network, was bigger than Claude's, the Standard Oil Network. Besides them, Phil Sutterfield did the UK games for WHAS in Louisville.

Even though I was the new guy on the block and the one

at the bottom of the totem pole, both Claude and J.B. were so damned good to me. It would have been natural for them to resent me, but they couldn't have been nicer. We made a lot of trips together, the three of us driving in the same car. I remember that somebody once remarked to Claude how surprising it was that the three of us could be so friendly and Claude said, "We only compete for an hour and a half on game nights." I thought that was fairly well put.

I have looked back on those years and thought so many times what good luck it was for me. J.B. and Claude were well established with their networks. Phil had the giant reach of the 50,000-watt WHAS. A listener could choose from among four different announcers doing the same game. That number grew to five when Dee Huddleston, who was later to become a U.S. Senator, started another network for Kentucky Central Insurance. Dee did the football season and Jim Host took over the play-by-play duties for the network when basketball rolled around. I say I was lucky because there's nothing like competition to make you work and make you sharp. I really had to hustle, and I've always been proud that in three years I went from the bottom of the totem pole in the ratings to second place. I think the competition did that for me.

I've always heard that the main reason Bryant left UK was because he was jealous of Coach Rupp. I don't know if that's true or not, but I do know that Rupp was the king — or "The Baron," as people called him because of his German ancestry — and he was in his heyday when I first came to Lexington. He had already won three NCAA championships — in 1948, '49, and '51 — and he would have probably had another one in 1952-53, except that the NCAA made UK cancel its season as punishment for recruiting violations and a few players' roles in the point-shaving scandals of the early 1950s. That made Coach Rupp furious, of course. He felt the NCAA was out to get him because he had grown so powerful, and he vowed that Walter Byers, then the executive director of the NCAA, would someday hand him another championship trophy.

I can remember the first time I met Coach Rupp as if it were yesterday. I called and told his secretary who I was and that I'd like to meet with Coach Rupp. She checked with him and came back and said he could see me for just a few minutes the next day. So I showed up in her little office the next day and she went in and said, "The fella from the radio station is here."

I heard him say, in that twang of his, "Well, have him come in."

I walked in and there he was — starched white shirt, blue tie. He had all these pictures in his office, and not many were basketball pictures. There were pictures of Bob Hope and Happy Chandler and even his Hereford cows. We shook hands and I remember thinking that he had the limpest handshake you could imagine for such a big, arrogant, self-assured man. But I was scared to death, let me tell you.

When I told him where I was from, he asked me if I knew Wallace Jones. Then he asked me if I'd ever seen the Coliseum, which was only three or four years old at the time. I had, but I lied to him and said I hadn't. So he took me for a tour, showing me the dressing rooms and everything. He was very proud of it. Later on, we were standing in the middle of the floor, and I noticed that the scoreboards had only two digits on them.

"Coach," I said, "I thought I'd read that you were going to add a third digit for all the big scores you planned on running up this year."

Well, he thought that was hilarious, and I began to feel at ease.

That season there was no question that UK had the best team in America. They opened against a good Temple team, and at halftime Cliff Hagan, UK's great center, had 20 points, the same as Temple. At the end Hagan was out there with four subs because Rupp wanted him to set the single-game scoring record. Finally, Linville Puckett threw a floor-length pass near the end of the game and Hagan laid it in. He had 51 points, a new record, and UK won 86-59. For a rookie announcer, that was quite an introduction to Wildcat basketball.

That team went on from there and just rolled. I'd rank it right up there with any team I've ever seen. In the finals of the first UK Invitational Tournament, UK beat La Salle and the great Tom Gola by 13 points. People forget what a tremendous basketball player Hagan was offensively. He wasn't much on defense because he didn't concentrate on it. He once told Frank Ramsey that "nobody makes All-American playing defense."

But he had the prettiest hook shot I've ever seen, with either hand, and from way out, too. And even though he was only 6'4", Cliff also was a tremendous rebounder. Just tough as hell. I remember UK was playing Auburn and one of the Auburn players made the mistake of trying to challenge Cliff. Next thing you know, here was the Auburn guy lying on the floor with his toes pointing to the ceiling. Hagan had done something terrible to him away from the ball. But he was quite a player. He's still the only guy I've ever seen who could tip the ball into the basket on a jump ball at the free-throw line.

Ramsey was such a slasher and driver that you could hear his shoes squeak when he cut. I remember that Coach Rupp once said, "Frank is the kind of player that if you win by 30, he'll get you three points, but if you win by three, he'll have 30." He was a great defensive player, too.

The third member of that team's Big Three was Lou Tsioropoulos. He was the blue-collar guy, the one who specialized in defense and rebounding. I remember that Harry Lancaster, who was Coach Rupp's assistant for so many years, first met him while Lou was traveling through Lexington on his way to Texas for an all-star football game. Lou wanted to try out for the UK basketball team but the floor in old Alumni Gym had just been painted. Harry called Coach Bryant and asked him if he'd take a look. Coach Bryant did, and he later called back to say, "If you don't want him, I do." That did it for Harry. The basketball team kept him.

Everything was going great until January 25, 1954, when Larry Boeck, who covered the team for *The Courier-Journal*, broke the story that Hagan, Ramsey and Tsioropoulos wouldn't be eligible for the NCAA Tournament because they were fifth-year graduate students. Back then the NCAA had a rule that graduate students could play during the regular season, but not during the tournament. Boy, you talk about an uproar! The people at UK were angry, naturally, but mostly embarrassed that they hadn't detected the problem themselves. Cliff told me later that Boeck and Harry Lancaster got into a fist fight over it.

Back then, you see, the writers who covered the team were very friendly, almost a part of the family. You didn't have a big budget for the sports information department because the writers did your PR work for you. When Boeck broke the story, a lot of UK people considered it a traitorous act. I'd say that was the beginning of the antagonism between UK and *The Courier-Journal*. There was no problem with the *Herald* and the *Leader* back then because Adolph and Fred Wachs, the *Herald's* and the *Leader's* publisher, were great buddies.

Despite Boeck's story, UK went on to finish the regular

season with a 24-0 record to become Rupp's first unbeaten team. In those days the Southeastern Conference had 12 teams and two divisions — they just went back to that in the 1991-92 season. Since Kentucky had not been permitted to play a schedule during the 1952-53 season, the conference decided that UK would pick up as if it had played the prior season. That meant the Wildcats would play each team in their own division twice, travel to three games in one division and have three from that division in Lexington. LSU refused to honor that arrangement, which would have sent them to Kentucky, claiming UK owed them a game. Instead of pairing Kentucky and LSU during the regular season, the SEC commissioner added Georgia to each team's schedule.

As it turned out, the Wildcats and Tigers went undefeated in conference play. On March 9, they had a playoff game in Nashville to determine the league champion and its representative in the NCAA. Back then, remember, a conference could send only one team to the tournament. LSU's star player was Bob Pettit, the big center who would later be Hagan's teammate on the St. Louis Hawks' NBA championship team of 1957-58.

Just before the game, here came Bernie Shively, UK's athletics director, with Coach Rupp, who was feeling so terrible that they had to help him up onto the elevated floor they have at Vanderbilt. Coach Rupp had suffered chest pains and was ordered to stay in bed the whole day. He didn't arrive at the gym until just before tipoff. Harry

Lancaster accompanied the team on the bus ride to Vandy's gym. Before the game, Cliff said, "Don't worry, Coach, we'll beat this bunch."

They did, but it turned out to be a whale of a game. At halftime UK led, 32-28, but LSU really got it cranked up in the second half and took a 40-36 lead when UK called time-out. In the huddle, as Ramsey later told me, Coach Rupp said, "By gawd, we're beat...get out there." But Lancaster told the players to go to a fullcourt press.

The score was tied, 46-46, after three quarters — yes, they played four 10-minute quarters back then — but suddenly Hagan and Ramsey took over the game. After UK took control, Rupp sent in Gayle Rose at guard for Puckett, and Rose, an expert ball-handler, killed the final minutes with a fantastic dribbling exhibition. The final score was UK 63, LSU 56. Ramsey had 30 points and Hagan 17 to lead the Wildcats, while Tsioropoulos held Pettit to 17, which was a little more than half his average.

In the dressing room, Rupp asked the squad to take a vote on whether UK should play in the NCAA Tournament without its three stars. Hagan, Ramsey and Tsioropoulos argued in favor of not going, on the grounds that the team would lose without them and have its perfect record spoiled. But with starting guard Billy Evans as their spokesman, the eligible players voted unanimously to go. The vote was 9-3. However, even as the vote was being taken in the locker room, Ken Kuhn, UK's sports information director, was passing out mimeographed sheets along the press table announcing that UK had decided not to go and was requesting the SEC to designate another team to represent the league. The hell with democracy; Coach Rupp had made up his mind.

As Ramsey later told me, Rupp came back into the locker room after the vote and said, "We're not going because I'm not going to take a bunch of turds like you to the NCAA."

Later, after a police escort had taken Rupp back to the Noel Hotel, the three seniors went to the coach's room and sat around talking. Adolph loved to lay in bed after a game, wearing those red pajamas and having a belt or two of Kentucky's finest bourbon. When Hagan, Ramsey and Tsioropoulos asked him what had been the secret of UK's first unbeaten season, Rupp snorted and said, "Hell, superior coaching!"

What a year! My first year at Kentucky and I had the honor of working with two of the giants in all of coaching history. Bear Bryant took the football team to a 7-2-1 record and defeated Tennessee for the first time in 17 years. Adolph Rupp took the basketball team to a perfect 25-0 record.

It doesn't get much better than that.

Chapter 3

Chasing The Bear's Legend

*T*here's no question that Bear Bryant gave UK its glory era in football, but he also ruined it for his successor, Blanton Collier. Before he left, Bryant put in a rule that Kentucky would recruit only five or six players from out of state. Some felt it was because he had lost Paul Hornung, the "Golden Boy" from Flaget High in Louisville who went on to win the 1956 Heisman Trophy at Notre Dame. Others felt the UK administration pressured him because it was embarrassed that so many of Bryant's players had come from out of state, including most of the great ones — Babe Parilli, Bob Gain, Steve Meilinger and many more. Under those restrictions, I really never understood why Collier took the job, because he was so hamstrung in recruiting.

I really got to know Collier very well because that's when WLEX got the coach's show. Collier was from Paris, Ky., which was also the home of Doug Gay and Guthrie Bell, who owned WLEX. Gay was a wealthy farmer and Bell was a soft-drink executive. In 1955, WLEX radio put WLEX-TV on the air, and I worked with Collier on both. It was sort of tough doing the show with Blanton, though, because even then he had a bad hearing problem and didn't do anything to help overcome it, such as using a hearing aid.

45

We had to get that volume really cranked up in the studio, but even then it was hard to communicate with him.

Collier was a coaching genius, one of the best students of the game I've ever known. Back then there was only one set of film on every game, so I had to go to Collier's house on Ridgeway Road every Sunday morning at 7 a.m. to sit there with the coaching staff while it graded the films. Collier was an absolute film fanatic. Just an expert. He noticed every little thing. He'd run that film back and forth and tell the backfield coach that his fullback was leaning the wrong way before the snap. That sort of thing. I learned a lot about football during those sessions. After the coaches broke up to go to church, I'd go down to the station to get the film ready for Collier's show.

Bryant left Collier with some pretty good players, and one of the best was Meilinger. He was so versatile that I believe he could have played any position on the field, on both sides of the ball. He almost did, as it was. On offense, he played quarterback, running back and end. On defense, he played end, linebacker and back. At one of the games, to emphasize how versatile he was, the band dressed up a trombone player in a football uniform with Steve's No. 80 on his jersey. A lot of people, even in the press box, thought it was really Steve.

Collier stayed around as long as he did mainly by beating Tennessee, something Bryant managed to do only once. In 1954, at the end of Collier's first season, he beat the Vols,

14-13, in Knoxville to finish up with a good 7-3 record. I remember Shields-Watkins field was a real mudhole that day. There are two plays from that game that I remember very well. With Tennessee leading, 13-7, Bradley Mills, UK's punter, was backed up to kick out of his end zone. After getting a bad snap, Mills, who was right-footed, did something I'd never seen before and haven't seen since — he booted it left-footed. He scooped up the low snap from center and took off in a dead run to his left and somehow was able to pause just long enough to get the kick away. Got it out about 35 yards, too.

Then there was the play in which quarterback Bob Hardy rolled out and found Howard Schnellenberger out in the left flat. Schnellenberger — who, by the way, had played with Paul Hornung at Flaget — blocked his man, then got up and found himself wide open. He just waltzed into the end zone for a touchdown. The extra point gave UK the win.

Another of Collier's wins over Tennessee that really sticks out in my mind came in 1957. After going 6-3-1 in 1955 and 6-4 in 1956, Collier's recruiting problems began to catch up with him and the Cats were only 2-7 going into that game. They were huge underdogs to a fine Tennessee team that had a fellow named Bobby Gordon at tailback.

The star of that game was big Lou Michaels, who may well be the best lineman ever to play at UK. Lou had a real mean streak in him. He's the only guy I've ever seen who loved practice because of the physical contact. But man, was he a player! He was a terrific blocker on offense and an incredible pass rusher on defense. Besides that, he also was the place-kicker. Best left-footed place-kicker in history, as he later proved during his pro career with the Baltimore Colts and Pittsburgh Steelers.

But getting back to that Tennessee game in Lou's senior year, Collier decided to put Michaels at middle linebacker, the only time in Lou's college career that he played there. You see, he was so awesome on defense that teams would always try to run away from his side of the line. Collier countered that by telling Lou not to line up until the offensive team had broken its huddle and shown its formation. That may have been the beginning of audibles, for all I know, because everybody playing UK would do anything to stay away from Michaels. But as I told you earlier, Collier was a master strategist, maybe the best X's and O's man UK has ever had, so he put Michaels at middle linebacker with no pass-coverage responsibility.

On Tennessee's first play from scrimmage, Michaels broke through, shook the ball loose and fell on it in the end zone. Then he kicked the extra point to give UK a 7-0 lead. Gordon, the Tennessee tailback, took Michaels' kickoff and was coming up the field when, at about the Tennessee 25, Michaels hit him like a runaway train. The ball must have gone 30 feet in the air and Jim Urbaniak recovered it for UK. The Wildcats scored again to go up 14-0 and that was it. The final score was UK 20, Tennessee 6, only because

Michaels missed the extra point after the third touchdown, his only miss of the year. The Associated Press named Michaels the national lineman-of-the-week and, boy, did he deserve it!

The next year the Cats went 5-4-1, beating Tennessee, 6-2, in a weird game in Knoxville. With Tennessee leading, 2-0, because UK's Calvin Bird had taken a safety, a guy named Carl Smith was trucking up the field for the Vols when UK's Jerry Eisaman, who played quarterback on offense and safety on defense, came up to him and just sort of bumped him. I didn't really see it, but somehow Eisaman plucked the ball away from Smith. The next thing you knew Eisaman was heading toward the end zone and Smith was chasing him. Smith caught Eisaman short of the goal line, but UK went on to score a few plays later.

The next three Collier teams went 4-6, 5-4-1 and 5-5, which just wasn't good enough to save his job. The fans had been spoiled by Bryant, and even though poor Blanton went 41-36-3, which is still the second-best winning percentage in UK history, a lot of people felt he just didn't measure up. Also, I remember there was a lot of criticism about his assistants, which seems like a joke when you think about it now. Six of Collier's assistants went on to become head coaches in the NFL — Don Shula, Chuck Knox, John North, Leeman Bennett, Bill Arnsparger and Schnellenberger. Whatever Blanton's problems were, his assistants had nothing to do with it. I'll always put the blame on the way he was handcuffed in recruiting. He got most of the good Kentucky players, but Kentucky has simply never produced enough quality players to win in the SEC. But even at that, it's easy to look back now and say that Blanton did a lot better job then he was given credit for.

After UK bought him out — and I don't think there was any question that the university had to make a change — Collier was hired to replace Paul Brown, his old mentor, with the Cleveland Browns, and doggone it if he didn't win the NFL championship in 1964. I wasn't surprised, because I knew how brilliant a football man Blanton was, but I was surprised by the way Brown turned his back on Blanton. He really got upset with Blanton for taking his old job and they never did make up. That's sad, because they were like brothers. I remember a lot of times, sitting around with Blanton, when he would begin a sentence by saying, "Paul Brown always said..." He just revered Brown.

It was during the Collier era that I had an opportunity to move to the big Ashland Oil Network to broadcast the games. During the spring meeting at Keeneland in 1955, J.B. Faulconer asked to ride from the track back to Lexington with me. On the way, he told me he planned to resign his job with Ashland to become Keeneland's first full-time publicist and he wanted to recommend me for his old position. He did and I met with two executives from WLAP, the flagship station for Ashland, at the old Lafayette Hotel in Lexington. They offered me the job, but they also offered me about half what J.B. was making and less than what I was being paid at WLEX. I turned them down on the spot.

The next year I left WLEX to move to WHAS in Louisville, the state's biggest and most powerful station. During the 1956 football season, I was offered the chance to go to station WAPI in Birmingham and do the Auburn games. Dan Daniels was leaving to do Washington Senators baseball and he recommended me to replace him. The very next day, WHAS called and offered me a job in the sports department. I drove to Louisville and met with George Walsh, who was then the sports director, and Sam Gifford in the old Brown Hotel grill. My income at the time was more than $8,300 a year and they offered me $6,500. I told 'em I'd have to think about it.

By the time Gifford called me four or five nights later, I'd already accepted an airline ticket to go to Birmingham. I told Sam that and he asked if I would call him when I returned with a yes or no on the WHAS offer. He called me back in an hour and offered me another $1,000 a year. I went to Birmingham and got a firm offer, but I came back and took the job at WHAS.

Why did I do it? Well, I had always wanted to work there. Because of the Bingham family that owned it, it was the epitome of a first-class operation. So I went to work there in early December of 1956. I did the first UK basketball game for WLEX and picked up the rest of the season for WHAS. I did get three pay raises that first year, so everything worked out well.

In my mind, I had a timetable as to where I wanted to be at various points in my career, and I must admit that I was a little ahead of schedule at that time. From a little station in Harlan to WHAS in five years — well, even now that would be a pretty good move. My career goal eventually had me working in New York, Chicago or some other major market, but that was before I knew how great it would be to work for the Binghams. Through the years, I was flattered that I was given the opportunity to work in New York, Chicago, St. Louis, Atlanta and those other markets, but I turned them all down.

In 1973, I think it was, I was offered the opportunity to be the voice of the Louisville Cardinals. Dave Hart, who was the athletics director at the time, called me and asked if he could stop by my office to discuss something he had in mind. I had known Dave since he was an assistant coach on Charlie Bradshaw's staff at Kentucky and always liked him a lot. He told me that Denny Crum had elevated the basketball program to a new level and that Louisville's entire sports program was on the move. He told me the program needed a first-class play-by-play man and he offered me the chance to join the athletics department at Louisville and to broadcast the Cardinal games. The figure Dave had in mind was barely half the income I was making at the time, so I had to say no. But it was certainly flattering to get the offer.

I'm not sure why I turned down all those other offers, but I sure am glad I did. Somehow, I just can't see myself being anything other than the "Voice of the Wildcats."

Chapter 4

The Fiddlin' Five

*E*ven though Kentucky had lost Hagan, Ramsey and Tsioropoulos after the 1953-54 season, Coach Rupp brought in Bob Burrow, a 6'7" junior college transfer, to play center, which helped the 1954-55 team get off to a fine start, winning its first seven games and earning the No. 1 ranking in the polls.

But then came January 8, 1955, a day that will live in infamy for UK fans. Georgia Tech came to town with a team that was just about the worst-looking one on UK's schedule. Really bad. Before the game, I met with color man Paul Cowley, a WLEX disc jockey, at a little chili parlor called "Benny's." We sat there having a bowl of chili and talking about the UK subs because we didn't think the starters were going to play very much against Tech.

Well, that's not exactly how it turned out. Whack Hyder, the Georgia Tech coach, was a colorful fellow who loved to try to get Coach Rupp's goat. But on this night, he really had his team ready to exploit Kentucky's overconfidence. Kentucky took the lead and held it through much of the game, but Tech wouldn't die. They just kept coming back and hanging around. At the end, UK was leading, 58-57, and Billy Evans had the ball. But a little Tech guard named Joe

Helms just took it away from Evans and hit a jump shot from about 10 or 12 feet. Time was running out, but Linville Puckett had the last shot for the Cats. It missed, and so did a tip-in attempt by Phil "Cookie" Grawemeyer as the final buzzer sounded. Final score: Tech 59, UK 58.

The thing I remember most is that the only noise in the Coliseum was the celebration of the Tech players, who had ended UK's winning streak of 32 games and its homecourt winning streak at 129, which is still the NCAA record. The Kentucky fans just sat there in a total state of shock. Some of them had never seen the Cats lose; remember, fans didn't go on the road in those days and none of the games were on TV. It had been 12 years since Kentucky had lost at home. The fans couldn't believe what they had seen, so they just sat there, frozen. Later, Coach Rupp told me that the two worst disasters in his lifetime were Pearl Harbor and that Georgia Tech game.

Well, Coach Rupp was so hot that he called a practice for the next day, a Sunday. Then he told the players he was taking away their tickets for the DePaul game Monday night. That did it for Puckett, who walked out of the meeting and later quit the team. So did Billy Bibb and Logan Gipe. All of them transferred to Kentucky Wesleyan in Owensboro. The team managed to get along without them, with its only other loss being to Georgia Tech again, this time by 65-59 on January 31 in Atlanta. They went into the 1955 NCAA Tournament as one of the favorites, but were upset by Marquette, 79-71, in the Mideast Regional in Evanston, Ill.

I think this is when it became obvious that the recruiting had begun to go downhill. For whatever reason, UK wasn't getting all the top high school players anymore, and many of those who did come didn't stay. Such talented players as Central City's Corky Withrow, Greenville's Roger Newman, Lone Jack's Bobby Slusher and Indiana's 1957 Mr. Basketball, Howard Dardeen, signed with UK, then departed.

As a quick fix, Adolph and Harry began going after junior college players. Burrow was the first, and he was followed by Adrian (Odie) Smith and Sid Cohen. Bennie Coffman was another junior college transfer who really helped the team. However, Bennie had transferred in as a regular student. It was after he was spotted playing well in an intramural league that he was invited to join the team. These players, along with some pretty good Kentucky kids, saved them during an era that was just so-so by UK standards.

The 1955-56 team went 20-6, but was beaten by Iowa and its All-American Carl (Sugar) Cain, 89-77, in the finals of the NCAA Midwest Regional on the Hawkeyes' floor in Iowa City. The next year, the NCAA Mideast Region was held right there in UK's Memorial Coliseum, but the Wildcats completed a 23-5 season by being upset by Michigan State and its fine center, Jumpin' Johnny Green, 80-68. Since both Cain and Green were black, this is when UK fans first became aware of the growing impact of the black athlete in college basketball. The SEC didn't have any black players in those days. In fact, the league was lily-white until the 1967-68 season, when Perry Wallace broke the color barrier at Vanderbilt.

Going into the 1957-58 season, UK's fans were growing restless. Some were even wondering if Rupp had lost his magic touch. Even Rupp didn't sound very optimistic as he looked over his players before the season. The starters were Johnny Cox, a skinny 6'4" forward from Hazard who was about as deadly a shooter, with both a jumper and a hook, as any forward in UK history; John Crigler, a tough senior rebounder and defensive specialist even though he was only 6'3"; Ed Beck, the raw-boned 6'7" center and ordained Methodist minister from Georgia who had tragically lost his wife, Billie, to cancer at the end of the previous season; Odie Smith, the tough little playmaker and set-shot artist; and Vernon Hatton, the 6'3" slashing senior guard from Lexington who was about as tough under pressure as any UK player ever. All were seniors except Cox, who was a junior. UK also had a deep bench that included players like Billy Ray Cassady, Don Mills and Lincoln Collinsworth. Yet before the season Rupp looked at them and said, "We're fiddlers, that's all. They're pretty good fiddlers — be right entertaining at a barn dance. But I'll tell you, you need violinists to play at Carnegie Hall. We don't have any violinists."

On December 7, 1957, that team and Temple, which was

led by the great Guy Rodgers at guard, played one of the most exciting games in UK history. After Hatton made a free throw to tie it up, Coach Rupp set up a play for Smith to take the last shot. He missed and the game went into overtime. Near the end of the first overtime, Temple was leading by two points with only one second remaining. During the UK timeout, you could hear all this noise. It was the crowd getting up and leaving, thinking Kentucky had no chance. Coach Rupp wanted Smith to once again take the last shot, but Harry Lancaster argued in favor of Hatton taking the shot. He hit a set shot from midcourt to tie it and send the game into a second overtime. By then the Coliseum was half-empty. But I guess a lot of people must have been listening on their car radios, because they started coming back in. By the time UK finally won, 85-83, in three overtimes, the place was full again.

That team managed to go on and win the SEC championship outright, but it needed to beat Tennessee in Knoxville in the last game of the season to do it. Rupp had benched Smith, but that night Odie earned his way back into the starting lineup by coming off the bench to lead UK to a 77-66 win. That gave the Cats a 19-6 record, their worst since 1940-41.

Still, I gave them a good chance in the NCAA Tournament for two reasons: all their games would be right here in Kentucky — the Mideast Regional was scheduled for the Coliseum and the Final Four for Freedom Hall in

Louisville — and the fact that the "Fiddlin' Five" was playing its sweetest music at just the right time. That team was
much better at the end of the year than it was at the beginning, as it proved in the regional by whipping Miami of
Ohio, 94-70, and then just crushing a really good Notre
Dame team, 89-56. The Irish were actually favored in that
game and they had a very good player in Tom Hawkins,
who had scored 31 against Indiana in the regional semifinal.
But Rupp ganged up on him, dropping Smitty back on him
in a double-team, and Hawkins got only 17 against the Cats.

So then it was on up the road to Louisville. Freedom
Hall was brand new back then and, with more than 19,000
seats for basketball, it was the biggest arena in the country.
I've always thought that right here is when the Final Four
began to turn into the monstrous event it has become. The
NCAA wasn't sure it could sell out an arena that big, but it
sold it out in '58 because Kentucky was in the Final Four
and again in '59 because Louisville was in the field. Bernie
Shively, the UK athletics director, deserved a lot of credit
for getting Freedom Hall the Final Four six times between
1958 and 1969. "Shive" was a member of the NCAA
Tournament Committee and was one of the most powerful
men in college basketball.

A Final Four record crowd of 18,586 showed up for the
semifinals on Friday, March 21, and doggone if UK's opponent wasn't the same Temple team the Cats had beaten in
triple-overtime back in December. This game was almost as

good as the first one, going right down to the wire before Hatton did it again, this time driving off a pick for a reverse layup that gave UK a 61-60 lead with 16 seconds to go. Before the Owls could get the ball to Rodgers for a potential game-winning shot, Temple's Bill "Pickles" Kennedy bobbled it out of bounds. Some people said Rupp should have used up more time before going for the final shot, but his reply was that you take a score anytime you can get it.

As exciting as that game was, however, everybody left the arena wondering how in the world UK could win the title. In the other semifinal, Seattle routed a tall, talented Kansas State team, 73-51, behind Elgin Baylor's 23 points and 22 rebounds. I wasn't the only one who thought Baylor was the best player I'd ever seen.

At the pregame meal on Saturday, Adolph and Harry hadn't come up with any plan to handle Baylor, so they sent the kids to bed. Then they went back to Adolph's room in the Seelbach Hotel, still trying to figure something out. Finally there was a knock on the door. The visitor was John Grayson, the coach at Idaho, and he had come to tell them how to beat Seattle. First, he said, Rupp had to keep the players from being mesmerized by Baylor, who was so flashy that he just made everybody want to stop and watch. And second, he said Baylor's only weakness was that he didn't play good defense against a driver. Adolph told Harry to get the kids out of bed so they could watch some film on Baylor. All of a sudden the coaches were excited because they had a game plan, and that made the kids excited.

When tipoff rolled around before a crowd of 18,803 — another record — Rupp was surprised to find that Seattle coach John Castellani had put Baylor on Crigler instead of Beck. The one thing Crigler did well offensively was drive, so that's what Rupp told him to do every time he got the ball. The result was three quick fouls on Baylor, which forced Castellani to take him off Crigler and put him on UK's low-scoring centers, Beck and backup Don Mills. Rupp countered that by ordering Hatton to drive the lane off picks set by Beck, which meant Baylor had to either risk further foul trouble or let Hatton score. When the frustrated Baylor picked up his fourth foul trying to block a Mills hook, it was over. Although Baylor had 25 points and 19 rebounds, Hatton scored 30 and Cox 24 as UK took an 84-72 victory and gave Coach Rupp his fourth NCAA title, a record that stood until UCLA won No. 5 for John Wooden in 1969.

The win over Seattle was a tremendous upset and it put UK back on top of the basketball world. Coach Rupp was very happy. One of the first people on the floor to hug him was his old friend Happy Chandler, then near the end of his second term as governor of Kentucky. Chandler was happy for two reasons — UK's championship and the big crowds. When he gave the go-ahead to build Freedom Hall, you see, he had been criticized for building a place so big. Some people said it would be a "white elephant." Anyhow, that championship meant a lot to Coach Rupp. At the banquet, he said: "These boys still are just a bunch of barnyard fiddlers, but they sure can fiddle!"

The only starter back the next season was Cox, and I remember what Coach Rupp did one day in practice after Cohen, one of the junior-college transfers, came down the floor several times in a row and worked the ball away from Cox. Rupp blew his whistle and walked out on the floor. "Sidney," he said to Cohen, "this is Johnny Cox. Last year Johnny made All-American and led us to the national championship. Sidney, I would appreciate it very much if you would pass the ball to Johnny." That was Coach Rupp at his funniest, sarcastic best.

I didn't really think they would have much of a team, but they surprised me by going 24-3. That was sort of a lucky 24-3, however. I remember a December game in the Coliseum in which Maryland had the Cats down by three with only seven seconds to play. There was no way for UK to win or even tie, because there wasn't a three-point shot. The Maryland coach told his players not to foul and just let UK score. Their first four players did exactly that but the fifth, a guy named Al Bunge, couldn't restrain himself. He fouled Bennie Coffman on a drive to send it into overtime. UK won, 58-56.

Another bit of luck for that team was that the state of Mississippi had a policy restricting any of its college athletic teams from playing against blacks. So even though

Mississippi State won the league championship, the Bulldogs declined the NCAA invitation — each league only got one back then, remember — and UK, the runner-up, got to go to Evanston, Ill., where its opening opponent was a solid Louisville team led by John Turner, a tough forward from Newport.

The Louisville fans were a lot more excited about the game than the UK fans because, to tell you the truth, those were the days when the Cards just weren't on the same level with the Cats. In fact, the UK players went into the game overconfident, and I'm sure that's what cost them the game. After UK jumped out to a big early lead, Louisville coach Peck Hickman did a good job of making some adjustments, mostly picking up UK's guards further out on the floor. The Cards pulled away for a 76-61 victory, the last time the teams played until the unforgettable "Dream Game" in the 1983 Mideast Regional in Knoxville.

I went back home to Louisville, where I did the Final Four play-by-play for what might have been the first radio network in NCAA Tournament history. There was no TV, of course, but WHAS had put together an 18-station radio network, all out-of-state and all big stations. Our sales manager, John Fouts, sold the whole network to General Electric, which offered to give the winning coach a new electric range. That coach turned out to be Pete Newell of California. After the Bears had beaten Jerry West and West Virginia, 71-70, in the title game, Bill Sheehy, who had been appointed to get the winning coach, went up to Newell and said, "Coach, I'm the man with the stove."

He brought Pete to me and I gave him the GE range.

Years later, while covering the Kentucky Derby, I ran into Pete outside trainer Wayne Lukas' barn at Churchill Downs. Bobby Knight, who is Pete's best friend, introduced us. I said, "The last time we met, Pete, I gave you a stove."

Believe it or not, Pete remembered that occasion. He also told me he had that stove until just a few years earlier. That just goes to show you how times have changed. Back then a basketball coach was glad to get a stove. Today they're making so much money they'd look at you as if you were crazy.

Chapter 5

The Bear's Second Coming...Sort Of

*A*fter getting rid of Blanton Collier, I think the university braintrust was looking to regain the Bear Bryant influence, which is why they hired Charlie Bradshaw. Charlie had been at UK before, both as a player under Bryant and an assistant under Collier, so they knew him well. They hired him off Bryant's staff at Alabama, where they were beginning to have all those national championships.

The Bradshaw who returned to UK as head coach was a different guy from the one I had known when he was an assistant. I think what happened to Charlie was what happened to a lot of former Bryant players and assistants. They wanted to be Bryant. So here was Charlie, with that deep voice like Bryant and all that talk about wanting to get kids who had "good mamas and papas." It was straight from the Bryant textbook.

Under Collier, the program had lost some discipline, no question about it, but Charlie tried too hard to turn that around. He put in an off-season "conditioning" program that was brutal. I remember they even had a throw-up barrel over there in the Shively Sports Center. By the time he got through practice in the spring of 1962, so many players had left, accusing Bradshaw of brutality, that *Sports Illustrated* even came in and did a story about it. The sad thing was a lot of the guys who quit were really good people. Dale Lindsey transferred to Western and went on to a distinguished pro career with the Cleveland Browns, Mike Minnix went on to become a successful physician and Jim Bolus became an outstanding turf writer in Louisville.

The '62 team, Bradshaw's first, came to be known as the "Thin 30," but it really had only 27 players. The players who stayed were really tough and aggressive. They went 3-5-2 on the season, but nobody blew 'em out and they beat Tennessee, 12-10, in Knoxville in their last game. Darrell Cox, the only one of the quitters that Bradshaw took back, had a big game against the Vols. The winning points came on a field goal by Clarkie Mayfield, who was to die a hero in the 1977 fire that destroyed the Beverly Hills Supper Club in Newport. Clarkie got out, but he went back in several times to help others before the fire finally got him. I've often wondered if his football training at UK had anything to do with that. He learned to live with pressure because nobody could put more pressure on you than Bradshaw.

All the negative publicity didn't hurt Bradshaw's recruiting. His first year at UK coincided with one of the few years in which Kentucky produced some really outstanding football players, and Bradshaw got them all — quarterback Rick Norton from Louisville Flaget, halfback Rodger Bird from Corbin, end Rick Kestner from Belfry, tackle Sam Ball from Henderson and linebacker Mike

McGraw from Ft. Thomas Highlands. As sophomores in 1963, they took their lumps on a team that was only 3-6-1, but they really elevated hopes when they were juniors.

After opening the 1964 season with an unimpressive victory over Detroit, Kentucky went to Jackson to play an Ole Miss team that was ranked No. 1 in the country. Nobody could have anticipated it before the game, but it turned out to be one of the biggest wins in UK history. In the early going, Kentucky twice drove into Ole Miss territory, but Norton was intercepted both times, one of which was returned for a Rebel touchdown. But then the Cats started clicking. Kestner had a big day, catching three touchdown passes, but I mostly remember a couple of halfback passes by Bird. On the first one, he hit Tom Becherer for a touchdown, but it was called back because UK had an ineligible receiver downfield. On the second, he hit Kestner for a TD. Neither one was a called play. Bird just improvised after seeing he had nowhere to go. Late in the game, Mike Dennis of Ole Miss caught a pass, but UK's Jimmy "Red" Foley really hit him, popping the ball loose so that Talbott Todd could catch it. The final score was UK 27, Ole Miss 21.

I remember Ole Miss coach Johnny Vaught coming into the Wildcats' locker room and telling the players it was the greatest exhibition he had ever seen. I thought that showed a lot of class. Later, when the team got back to Lexington, there were so many people at the airport — about 20,000, by one estimate — that the plane couldn't even taxi all the way to the terminal.

Next up for Kentucky was a good Auburn club that inherited the No. 1 spot in the rankings after Ole Miss lost. Kentucky clobbered Auburn, 20-0, and moved into the Top 10 for the first time since I began calling the games. Finally, it looked as if Bradshaw had it going. But then the team went to Tallahassee and got bombed by Florida State, 48-6. They just couldn't stop quarterback Steve Tensi and his ace receiver, Fred Biletnikoff, who went on to have a great pro career. Bradshaw was so upset that he really bore down on them, and they weren't the same team after that. What had promised to be a breakthrough season turned out to be only 5-5, the same record that had gotten Collier fired after the '61 season.

Nevertheless, hopes were sky-high heading into the 1965 season. The team got off to a decent start, winning six of its first eight games. The game I remember most was a 16-7 win over Ole Miss under the lights at Stoll Field. Larry Seiple, who was then a junior, had dropped back to punt with the Cats hanging on to a 9-7 lead. It was fourth and 41, or something weird like that, and UK was on its own 30. But for some strange reason, Ole Miss didn't rush. Seiple hesitated. He looked like he was going to run, then he looked like he wasn't. Finally he took off. It was strange to see all those Ole Miss players running with their backs to him as if they were his blockers. But he took it all the way, and that broke the game open.

Going into their game at Houston with a 6-2 record and one of the most explosive offenses in the nation, the Cats had a bid to the Gator Bowl in their paws. However, Bradshaw decided to gamble for bigger stakes. He wanted to go to the Cotton Bowl, and a win over Houston would guarantee that. The team went into the game as a 21-point favorite and so confident of victory that Bradshaw even took along the university president, Dr. John Oswald, so he could officially accept the Cotton Bowl invitation after the game.

Well, the Cats led, 21-16, at halftime, but then Houston fought back to get the lead in the third quarter. The outcome was still in doubt when Norton, the team's indispensable player, hurt a knee and had to be removed from the game. That was it. Houston won, 38-21, and the Cats dropped out of the bowl picture. Without Norton, they had no offense. The next week, with safety Terry Beadles playing quarterback, they lost at home to Tennessee, 19-3. I thought that was very unfair to Beadles, who hadn't played quarterback all year. That was an awfully good team to go 6-4, and I think that's when Charlie's program was cooked.

Charlie had loaded his offensive unit, the result being a quick-strike potential unequalled by any team I've covered at UK. Norton might have been the best quarterback in the past 39 years. He had the incredible ability to throw perfect strikes at long range. Bird was a darting, dipsy-doodle runner who created pure excitement. Ball was a big bear of a tackle who could really open the holes. Despite a 6-4 record, all three of them were named to the All-America team. Along with those three, Rick Kestner, Doug Davis, Larry Seiple and Bob Windsor were also excellent players.

One game that season showed just how explosive that team could be on offense. It was the Georgia game at Stoll Field. Trailing 10-0 at the end of the first quarter, the Wildcats struck for four touchdowns in the second quarter for a 28-10 halftime lead. The game ended with that same score.

Charlie's last three teams went 3-6-1 in 1966, 2-8 in 1967 and 3-7 in 1968. About the only thing they had going for them during that time was Dicky Lyons, who may be the toughest kid who played at UK during my 39 years. He wasn't very big or very fast, but he may be the best punt and kickoff return man the Cats have ever had. He started off as a defensive back, but he played fullback, tailback and quarterback — and played them all well. In his junior year in 1967, he scored all the points in a 22-7 win over West Virginia in Lexington — three touchdowns, an extra point and a field goal. He was an intense competitor, tough as a pine knot. Once he got so disgusted after dropping a ball that he kicked it into the stands.

Dickie was just as intense in practice as he was in a game. One day when a big sophomore fullback named Raynard Makin kept fouling up, Lyons walked up behind him and booted him right in the fanny to send him sprawling. Makin took his punishment meekly. He may have been the bigger man, but he wanted no part of Lyons.

I recall one year when Kentucky went down to play Florida, a newspaper man quoted Bradshaw as saying, "I don't know where we'd be without Lyons." The reporter wrote that he could easily provide Charlie with the answer. He said without Lyons, instead of being 2-6, UK would be 0-8. If Charlie had had a few more like him, he might have made it.

Right before the West Virginia game in 1968, Charlie told the team he had decided to resign. They went out and beat the Mountaineers, but the Cats lost their last three. That was it for Charlie. I'll always wonder if it might have been different if he had just tried to be himself instead of trying to be the second coming of the Bear.

In 1967, Charlie's next-to-last year, the team got beat by Auburn, 48-7, and the week after that was the first time I was ever confronted by a coach. We were over at the Shively Sports Center and Charlie said, "Can I see you a minute?"

I followed him into the locker room and we sat there, straddling a bench and looking at each other.

"Why are you against us?" he said.

"I'm not against you."

"Well, people have told me that you were negative during the Auburn game," he said.

"When you get beat 48-7," I told him, "I don't have the talent to make you sound good."

I told Charlie that I couldn't be against Kentucky and that I hoped the Wildcats won every year. I told him I just couldn't get into calling Kentucky "we" and the other team "they." He wanted to know why not. There was nothing more to say.

I thought that might be the end of my UK career right there. I was afraid he might try to get me fired. I was so concerned that I went to Bernie Shively, the athletics director. I'll never forget what he told me. "I picked you," he said, "and I'll tell you when to go. As far as I'm concerned, you'll be around here a long time."

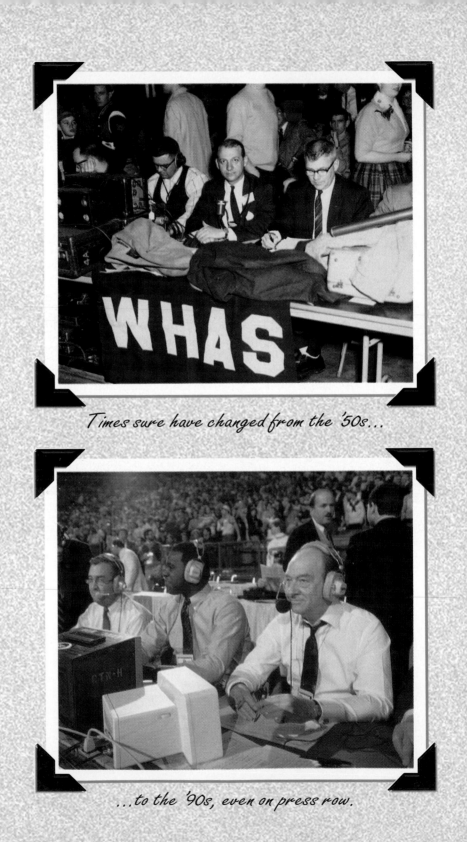

Times sure have changed from the '50s...

...to the '90s, even on press row.

Baby Cawood

The graduate

Cawood (left), with Jess Clem, got
an early start in the horse business.

The horseman (above) and dancing the night away (right) at Centre College.

The President of Centre's Intrafraternity Council (front and center).

Cawood during his stint in the Marines.

A man in uniform.

PLATOON 583 U.S. MARINE CORPS
SAN DIEGO
1944
U.S. MARINES SEMPER FIDELIS

Platoon 583, U.S. Marines '44 (Cawood is number 35)

The Voice of the Wildcats

The young broadcaster with Bernie Shively (left) and Ken Kuhn (right).

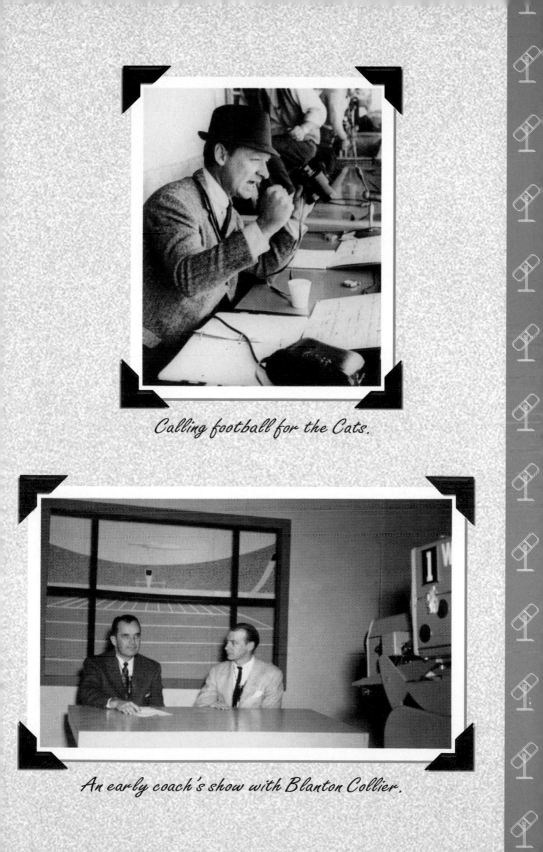

Calling football for the Cats.

An early coach's show with Blanton Collier.

Another brush with stardom — this time Burt Lancaster.

Cawood interviewing PGA golfer Bobby Nichols.

Cawood's TV golf show with Frank Atkins.

Speaking with legendary jockey Eddie Arcaro (center).

From behind the microphone to behind the trotter.

Filming a special with Cassius Clay.

Cawood with another heavyweight champ — Joe Louis.

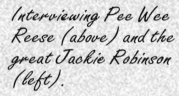

Interviewing Pee Wee Reese (above) and the great Jackie Robinson (left).

Talking baseball with Charlie Hustle himself, Pete Rose.

Cawood having some
fun with Oscar
Combs and Earl Cox
(above) and Ralph
Hacker (left).

The honorary coach of the Playboy
Bunnies (with Lee Corso) in 1971.

Cawood and Joe B.
Hall filming a TV
interview (above)
and clowning around
off camera (left).

With Kyle Macy.

Cawood with the legendary Adolph Rupp.

With Rupp assistant and, later, UK athletics director Harry Lancaster.

Cawood with his mother, Sudie.

Cawood and Frances in the spotlight.

Chapter 6

Rupp's Runts

I 've never understood why Cotton Nash took so many knocks from the fans. Even though he was a three-time All-American, he was never able to satisfy everyone. Maybe that's a tribute, in a back-handed way, because it tells you the kind of expectations he generated. As far as I'm concerned, they ought to build a monument to the guy. After UK had gone 19-9 in 1960-61, he absolutely carried the program on his back for the next three years.

Oh, they had some good kids who tried hard in those days. Larry Pursiful, who was two years ahead of Cotton, was an outstanding shooter and one of the most underrated players to ever wear Kentucky blue and white. Scotty Baesler, a year ahead of Nash, showed the kind of leadership that later enabled him to become mayor of Lexington. And I remember guys like Ted Deeken, Allen Feldhaus, Carroll Burchett, Roy Roberts and Terry Mobley. All of them gave it everything they had. But without Nash, those would have been lean years at UK. The recruiting had gone bad. No longer was UK at the pinnacle of college basketball. The pendulum had swung to Ohio, which produced three-consecutive national champions (Ohio State in 1960, Cincinnati in '61 and '62), and to California, where UCLA's titles in

1964 and '65 were the beginning of the John Wooden dynasty.

A lot of the unhappiness with Cotton came from Coach Rupp. Harry Lancaster told me once that after the team had lost to Ohio State in the NCAA Mideast Regional finals at the end of Cotton's sophomore year, he and Coach Rupp read Cotton the riot act, telling him he was a gutless player who couldn't produce against the good teams. They probably shouldn't have done that, in retrospect, because it might have ruined him.

The truth be told, they were being unfair to Cotton, making him play center at 6'5" when he should have been at guard. He was a classic 'tweener — a little too small to play up front, but too big to be in the backcourt. But my, could he play. Teams had a hard time guarding him man-to-man because he would take smaller players inside and bigger players outside. One year when Auburn had a real good defensive center named Layton Johns, Coach Rupp isolated Cotton and Cotton ate Johns alive.

At the beginning of Cotton's senior year, three very gifted sophomores moved up to the varsity and things were looking bright again in the Kentucky camp. Coach Rupp called them the "Katzenjammer Kids" from an old comic strip. They were Larry Conley, Tommy Kron and Mickey Gibson. Conley moved right up to the starting five as a sophomore. Kron and Gibson were valuable reserves. Conley and Kron were to have great careers at UK, but

Gibson, a talented left-hander out of Hazard, ran into disciplinary problems and left the university.

The 1963-64 season, Cotton's senior year, ended when the Cats were upset in the Mideast Regional by an Ohio University team that was built around a couple of fine black players. It was obvious then that blacks were having more and more of an impact on the game, and Dr. Oswald was after Coach Rupp to recruit the best black kids in Kentucky. They really wanted Wes Unseld, who led Louisville Seneca High to a second consecutive state tournament championship in 1964, but I don't think Wes really wanted to be a pioneer. He would have been the perfect player to integrate the program. Put him at center on the "Runts" and they'd have been unbeaten.

Conley and Kron were sophomores on Nash's last team, and the next season they were joined on the varsity by a couple of sophomores named Pat Riley and Louie Dampier. Nevertheless, that 1964-65 team went only 15-10, the worst record of Coach Rupp's career up to that point. All over the state you heard people saying that Rupp just didn't have it anymore, that maybe he should think about retiring. After that season, Rupp brought back Joe B. Hall, who had played briefly for him in the late 1940s, as an assistant. One of the first things Hall did was put in an off-season conditioning program. UK had never had that before, and I think that had a lot to do with making the next season's team as good as it was.

Going into that 1965-66 season, the prospects looked bleaker for UK than they had in years. Conley, Kron, Riley and Dampier were back, but so what? Who could get excited about having four starters back from a 15-10 team? And in the pivot, replacing John Adams, was Thad Jaracz, a left-handed sophomore from Lexington Lafayette who still had some baby fat on him. None of the starters was taller than 6'5". They weren't picked in the Top 25 of anybody's poll, probably not even the Top 50, but they became Coach Rupp's favorite team by making one of the greatest turn-arounds in basketball history.

The most important aspect of that team was the unselfishness of Conley and Kron, the seniors who sacrificed their scoring for the good of the team. Mainly because of them, "Rupp's Runts," as they came to be known, were the best passing team in my years at Kentucky. In addition, they played the 1-3-1 trapping zone defense about as well as it can be played. Of course, Coach Rupp, who always played man-to-man, refused to call it a zone. After he had used it to beat Tennessee in Knoxville the previous season, he said, with a straight face, that it wasn't a zone but a "hyperbolic transitional stratified parabola."

Well, the "Runts" won 23 in a row before losing to Tennessee in Knoxville. I can remember Tennessee coach Ray Mears saying that he had done Kentucky a favor by getting the monkey off its back. The team finished the regular season with a 24-1 record and went into the NCAA

Tournament ranked No. 1 in the country. Even then it was obvious that Coach Rupp loved that team, as did the whole state. I think he loved it because of the way it played, certainly, but also because it brought him back into the limelight and reminded the nation that he wasn't washed up yet.

The team went to Iowa City, Iowa, to play Dayton in the semifinals of the Mideast Regional. The other game was between Michigan, which had lost to UCLA in the championship game the previous season, and Western Kentucky, which had a fine team built around Clem "The Gem" Haskins. After Western had ripped a fine Loyola of Chicago team to earn the right to play in Iowa City, everybody figured the Mideast championship would be an all-Kentucky shootout.

It would have been, too, except that Western got beat on a horrendous jump-ball call by referee Steve Honzo. He called a foul on Western's Greg Smith instead of Michigan's great Cazzie Russell, and that put the Wolverines into the title game against UK, which had a fairly easy time with Dayton. I'll always be sorry that UK and Western didn't get to play because it would have been a terrific matchup. Western wasn't real big either, and Haskins was such a great player. The "Runts" had an easier time with Michigan than they would have had with the Hilltoppers, winning, 84-77, to advance to the Final Four in College Park, Md.

Going in, UK was ranked No. 1 and Duke No. 2, and everybody figured their meeting in the semifinal would be the real national championship game. The other semifinal-ists, Texas Western and Utah, weren't given much of a chance. Even though Conley had the flu, the Cats beat Duke, 83-79, in a helluva game. Riley hurt his foot that night, but didn't tell anybody until the next evening when the team was on the way to the arena to play Texas Western, which had eliminated Utah. Even so, just about everybody figured that the "Runts" were destined to win Rupp his fifth NCAA title.

But the Wildcats lost, 72-65, in what was the biggest disappointment of Coach Rupp's career. Later, a lot of sports writers made a big deal out of the fact that an all-black team had defeated an all-white team, but that wasn't much of an issue at the time. I think it was simply a combination of things. Texas Western was quicker, UK wasn't 100 percent physically and I think the Wildcat players thought, as most people did, that the Duke game had been the real champi-onship.

Coach Rupp really took it hard, possibly harder than any loss in his 42 years as the UK coach. It had been just an incredible ride for him that year, and I don't think he was consoled much by the huge crowd that greeted the team in the Coliseum when it returned from College Park. Conley spoke for the players and he was all choked up when he said, "We did the best we could."

I'll always have a soft spot in my heart for those five guys, each of whom played his role perfectly.

Although Kron, at 6'5", was really the tallest man in the lineup, he started all the plays, much like a point guard today, and played the point in the 1-3-1. He, like Dampier, had outstanding shooting range. I remember one year when Alabama coach Hayden Riley had given UK fits by playing a diamond-and-one, with the chaser on Dampier. Thinking Hayden would do the same thing when UK came to Tuscaloosa, Coach Rupp pumped up Kron and told him he would have to do more scoring. Well, Alabama didn't open in the diamond-and-one, but Kron didn't notice. He got the opening tip, took a few dribbles past midcourt, and let it fly. Coach Rupp stood up and stomped his foot. He quickly sat back down when the ball hit nothing but the bottom of the net.

Conley was an old gym rat whose father George had been a coach and later a well-known official in the SEC. Larry was one of the smartest players I've ever seen. He was 6'3" and frail, but he was a surprisingly good rebounder. He also was a great defensive player because he had such good anticipation and instincts. He was the best passer on the team, and one of the most underrated players in UK history.

Riley was the best athlete on the team. He might have been an even better football player than he was a basketball player. When he was in high school, Bear Bryant personally flew up to Schenectady, N.Y., to see him and recruit him to be a quarterback. But Pat wanted to play basketball and that turned out to be a wise choice. Although he was only 6'3", he jumped center for the "Runts" and got most of the taps. He could really jump, he played the baseline in the 1-3-1 and he was a good shooter with plenty of range. The funny thing is, I never thought about Pat becoming a coach, but with that great run he had with the L.A. Lakers in the 1980s, he only proved that you never know where good coaches might come from.

Dampier is one of the best, if not the best, long-range shooters who's ever played at the university. He was so automatic that Coach Rupp used to have a saying: "That's two for Lou." One year Vanderbilt tried to zone Louie and he ripped them for 42. Although he didn't have great foot speed, he was a better defensive player than most people knew. It took his pro career, all those great years with the Kentucky Colonels and the San Antonio Spurs, to show us what a tough little guy he was. He was tough as hickory. He loved the game and always was in great condition.

That leaves Jaracz, who was quicker than he looked. He had this little old dinky hook, but he could sure hit it. The other four older players sort of took care of Thad, who played in the middle, but he could score when they got the ball to him. He looked so unorthodox that you wouldn't want to use any of his shots in a coaching clinic, but he could put it in. He always was there to take advantage when teams tried to gang up their defenses on Pat and Louie.

The "Runts" came back to Lexington and were introduced before a game in Rupp Arena in 1991, the 25th anniversary year of their run to glory. The crowd almost tore the roof down, especially when Riley was introduced. Too bad Coach Rupp couldn't have been there. He really loved that team. So did I.

Chapter 7

Rupp's Last Hurrah

*T*he great run by the "Runts" created high expectations for the 1966-67 season. Conley and Kron were gone, but Dampier, Riley and Jaracz were back. During the summer, however, Riley had injured his back while water-skiing and nobody knew it until practice started. Coach Rupp really would have liked to hold Riley out for a year, but he couldn't afford to do it. As it turned out, the season went pretty much according to how Riley's back felt. When Pat was okay, it was a decent team. But when he wasn't, the team really struggled. There were times when his back was so bad that he couldn't even bend over to pick up a ball.

It was a tough year, all the way around. Coach Rupp always took pride in his teams' ability to win the close ones, but this team played four overtime games and lost them all. Then at mid-season, guard Bob Tallent, a pretty good player from Maytown, mouthed off to Coach Rupp after being pulled from a game in Knoxville, and the next day Adolph kicked him off the team. They really needed Tallent, but nobody mouthed off to Coach Rupp and got away with it.

They were 12-13 going into the final game of the season, and needed to beat Alabama to avoid giving Coach Rupp his first losing record. Luckily for the Cats, Riley was feeling good that night. He scored 28 in his final game and Kentucky rolled to a 110-78 win.

One night in December of that season, Bernie Shively told me to meet with him under the stands at the Coliseum to have a talk. "As you know," he told me, "every team in the SEC has gone to an exclusivity on its radio broadcasts except us. The reason we haven't is that I wasn't willing to give up either you or Claude Sullivan. But Claude's sick, so we're going to exclusivity next year and I want you to be the announcer."

I didn't know how to react. I knew Claude was ill — he died in December, 1967 — but I didn't know if WHAS would go for it. They were very provincial in those days. When I mentioned that to Shive, he said, "You leave that to me — do you want to do it or not?"

"Hell, yes," I said.

About a month later, Vic Sholis, who was my boss at WHAS, called and asked if I could come to his office. Well, you're darned right I could. When the general manager of the station wants to see you, you hop. When I got there, Sholis was sitting with Shive and Glenwood Creech, who was a UK vice president. "Do you want to be the voice of the Wildcats?" Sholis asked.

By then I realized Shive already had gotten the job done, and the next season UK went to exclusivity with me as the only play-by-play man.

The first network rights were owned by G.H. Johnston,

an outfit out of New York, and the funny thing was, they wanted it mainly for football, not basketball. I remember having dinner with their agent, a guy named Dick Frick, at the Campbell House. He told me they had agreed to take basketball to get football, which tells you right away that he was an out-of-towner. I told him, "Around these parts, basketball is the thing people care about the most."

The first year I was the sole voice of the Wildcats, the basketball team had the so-called "Super Sophs" who had gone 18-2 as freshmen. Mike Casey of Shelby County and Mike Pratt from Dayton, Ohio, both were sensational prospects, but the guy who really had people excited was Dan Issel. At 6'9", he figured to be UK's best center prospect since Bill Spivey in the early 1950s. This is when Joe B. Hall's recruiting had started to kick in. Adolph hadn't done much for years and Harry Lancaster had lost his zest for the chase. But Hall was eager and effective. After he failed to get his first two center prospects that year — George Janky from Ohio and a guy named Dick Broderson from Iowa — Hall managed to get Issel away from Wisconsin, which already had signed him to a national letter-of-intent.

I got my first hint of how good Issel might be when I ran into John Dromo, the Louisville assistant, before a Kentucky-Indiana high school all-star game in Louisville. I asked him about Issel and he said, "Janky can't carry Issel's shoes." Sure enough, when the Kentucky freshmen played the Dayton freshmen, Issel beat Janky like a drum.

They opened the 1967-68 season by beating a good Michigan team — which had an outstanding sophomore of its own named Rudy Tomjanovich — on the road, 96-79. When we got back home, however, there was bad news: Bernie Shively had died.

Shive was one of my all-time favorite characters. He used to like to play cards better than anyone I ever saw. When we'd be going somewhere on a plane, he and Jim Host would be playing gin rummy before they'd get the wheels up on the plane. He also was the guy who organized the poker games on the road. At about 6'5" and 250 pounds, Shive was a huge bear of a man. He had played football with Red Grange at Illinois, where he also was the Big Ten wrestling champion. He told me once that he never competed against anybody who was bigger than he was. He had a heart to match his body, too. Just a really sweet, kind man.

As the '67-68 season unfolded, it was Casey, more than Issel, who was the team's star. The Cats got off to a 9-1 start, lost three of four during a stretch of SEC play, and then won 11 in a row to take a 21-4 record into the NCAA Tournament. During the latter stage of the season, Issel began to mature. On January 15, with 15 minutes left in a 104-73 win over Georgia in the Coliseum, Issel went over a Georgia player's back and hit his head on the floor, suffering a mild concussion. That was the night he scored zero points and got only two rebounds while Georgia's center, Bob

Lienhard, was getting 29 points and 12 rebounds. That game seemed to serve as a wake-up call for Dan, and he joined with Casey to give UK a potent one-two punch down the stretch that season.

With the Mideast Regional being held in the Coliseum, it was hard for UK fans to avoid thinking a trip to the Final Four in Los Angeles was in the bag. Coach Rupp already had become the winningest coach in history that season, surpassing the 760 games won at Kansas by his old coach, Dr. Phog Allen. But he also wanted to get to the Final Four to prevent UCLA's John Wooden from tying his record of four national titles. That season the Bruins had the game's most devastating player — 7'2" junior Lew Alcindor. It was hard to see how anybody except Houston had much of a chance. During the regular season, the Cougars had used a great game by their All-American, Elvin Hayes, to upset UCLA in a nationally televised shootout in the Astrodome.

Kentucky's first opponent in Lexington was Marquette, coached by Al McGuire. Back in those days, McGuire wasn't always the loveable, funny guy that fans came to know through his analyst job with NBC. When he came to Lexington that year, in fact, he tried his darnedest to upset Coach Rupp and get his goat. First he refused to join the other regional coaches on Coach Rupp's TV show. Then he complained about everything. He said he wanted to sit on the home team's bench, wear the home uniforms and be the home team on the scoreboard. That was all show, of course, because the NCAA Tournament rules stipulated that UK got all those things. And Coach Rupp got in the last shot when McGuire balked at playing with a basketball that had Rupp's signature on it. "We'll play with one with your name on it," Coach Rupp said, "if you can find one."

Well, what all this did was get the Kentucky team and the crowd really fired up. McGuire had promised that his center would get the opening tip against Issel, but Dan got it and the Cats were on the way to a 107-89 romp. They just killed Marquette. The trouble was, they also killed their chances of going to the Final Four. They were so sky-high for Marquette that they came out flat the next night and lost to a very ordinary Ohio State team, 82-81, when a guy named Dave Sorenson hit a shot at the end. It didn't help Coach Rupp's disposition any when UCLA went on to win Wooden his fourth title.

That turned out to be Harry Lancaster's last season as Adolph's assistant. He was named acting athletics director and later got the job on a permanent basis. Adolph and Harry had been very close, but after Harry became Adolph's boss they became estranged. It got to the point where they didn't speak until 1977, when Coach Rupp was dying in the hospital. Harry told me that the final straw came one day when he heard Adolph out in the hall in the Coliseum, making disparaging remarks about something to do with the athletics department. Harry said he ignored it as long as he could, but he finally called Adolph in and said, "When I was your assistant, I was very loyal to you, but now I'm your boss and I expect you to be loyal to me."

Harry told me later that he regretted doing that because he and Adolph just stopped talking to each other.

The 1968-69 season is when Issel emerged as a scoring machine. His 26.6 average that season was a UK record, and the Cats rode him to a 22-4 record heading into the NCAA Tournament. This time the Mideast Regional was held in Madison, Wis., and waiting there, eager for revenge, was Al McGuire and Marquette. Al later said he used race to fire up his all-black team to play all-white Kentucky. "It was the worst thing I ever did in coaching," he said.

The Warriors were so fired up that, as the game wore on, McGuire became afraid that somebody might snap and start a fight. At one point, a Marquette player and a Kentucky player squared off, but it was broken up before any blows could be thrown.

McGuire's strategy was to double-team Issel and not guard Larry Steele. It worked well enough for the Warriors to score an 81-74 upset. Afterward, McGuire made his players shake hands with the Kentucky players. That year's NCAA title was again won by UCLA, giving Wooden his record fifth.

Going into the 1969-70 season, however, Kentucky figured to have a tremendous chance at getting No. 5 for Coach Rupp. Alcindor finally was gone from UCLA and the Wildcats had Issel, Casey and Pratt returning for their senior seasons. But during the summer, Casey broke his leg in an automobile accident, putting him out for the year. That was a terrible blow to Kentucky's title hopes. Casey was one of those gym rats who had a great nose for the ball. He also was a heckuva clutch player. Without him, UK would have to depend even more on Issel, who responded magnificently by averaging 33.7 points, still the school record.

There were some great scorers in college ball that season — Issel, Calvin Murphy of Niagara, Austin Carr of Notre Dame. But the best was "Pistol" Pete Maravich of LSU, who became the NCAA's all-time scoring champion. He was coached by his father, Press, who gave him the green light to shoot at will, just as Rupp had done with Issel at UK. In the six games he played against UK, Maravich never beat the Cats, but he turned every game into showtime. One of the great scoring duels in college history came when UK played LSU in Baton Rouge on February 21, 1970. The Pistol went for 64 and Issel for 51 as UK won, 121-105. Earlier that month, Issel scored 53, still the UK record, against Ole Miss. He could have scored even more against the Rebels, but Coach Rupp pulled him with a lot of time remaining.

This was the year Joe Hall quit and left to take the head coaching job at St. Louis. Hall left for one reason...because Coach Rupp wouldn't promise to support him when the UK coaching job did open up. But Harry Miller, a Lexington attorney, and Albert Clay, a prominent horseman, flew out to

St. Louis and got Joe to come back by telling him they would support him whenever Rupp left. Nevertheless, that led to a strained relationship between Adolph and Joe.

Later in the season, Joe was involved in another incident that might well have cost the team the 1970 national title. While the team was in Starkville, Miss., on a Sunday night, Joe and Claude Vaughn, the team's trainer, caught guard Bob McCowan and forward Randy Pool drinking beer at a place outside of town called the Crossroads. They reported the two to Coach Rupp, and he kicked both of them off the team. I remember McCowan and his mother, who had made the trip, leaving town the next morning on a plane. Mike Pratt later said the loss of McCowan probably cost the team the title because he was UK's best guard in the absence of Casey. I always liked the line by a writer from Knoxville who said, "Hell, anybody who could find a beer in Starkville on a Sunday night should be rewarded, not punished."

Going into the NCAA Mideast Regional with a 25-1 record and No. 1 ranking in the polls, the Cats beat Notre Dame, 109-99, in the semifinals to set up a regional championship against Jacksonville. The Dolphins had a pair of seven-footers, Artis Gilmore being by far the better of the two, and a fine big guard named Rex Morgan. But the guy who won the game for them was Vaughn Wedeking, their little point guard. After Issel had picked up his fourth foul, Wedeking sneaked into Issel's path as he was heading up the floor. Big Dan had his head turned, and when he ran into

Wedeking, the officials called him for his fifth foul. I thought that was a real chicken call. The team played hard without Dan, but it just couldn't beat Jacksonville without him, and finally lost, 106-100. The Dolphins went on to the NCAA title game, where they lost to a so-so UCLA team, giving Wooden title No. 6.

Although Casey came back for his senior year in 1970-71, he was never the player he had been before the accident. Issel's replacement was 7'1" Tom Payne, Rupp's first black player. Payne was thought to be a project when he joined the varsity. For one thing, he had developed late in his career at Louisville Shawnee High. Then, instead of being able to play for UK's freshman team, he was forced to play on an AAU squad that winter because he wasn't academically eligible for a scholarship. Nevertheless, he developed quicker than anybody expected and had moments where he was the dominant force in a game. His 16.9 average was third on the team, behind Tom Parker's 17.6 and Casey's 17.0, and the Wildcats took a surprisingly good 22-4 record into the Mideast Regional in Athens, Ga., where their first opponent was none other than Western Kentucky.

The Hilltoppers were sky-high for the game. One reason was Rupp's policy against scheduling other teams from the state. Another was that all five of Western's starters — Jim McDaniels, Clarence Glover, Jerome Perry, Jim Rose and Jerry Dunn — were blacks from Kentucky who knew that UK had been the last major program in the state to integrate its team. But emotion aside, Western was just a darned sight better than UK. In fact, that may have been Western's best team ever, even better than the Clem Haskins-Dwight Smith bunch of 1966. The Hilltoppers won, 107-83, and went on to beat Ohio State to earn a trip to the Final Four in Houston. Once again, however, the national title went to UCLA, Wooden's seventh. Before the next season, Payne declared hardship and entered the NBA draft, where the Atlanta Hawks picked him.

Going into the 1971-72 season, there was a lot of confusion and controversy over whether it would be Coach Rupp's last season. He turned 70 that season, the university's mandatory retirement age, and UK president Dr. Otis Singletary had made it clear that he wasn't going to make an exception for his basketball coach. Instead of accepting this meekly, however, Coach Rupp decided to go above Singletary's head and take his case to the public. He figured that if he could rally enough support Singletary would be forced to back down.

So from the beginning, the season had a soap-opera quality about it. Coach Rupp perceived Joe Hall as his only rival for the job, so he pretended that Joe wasn't alive, instead promoting a new assistant, Gale Catlett, at every opportunity because he knew Catlett was no threat. Everybody was forced to choose sides. The Browns, John Y. Sr. and John Y. Jr., both sided with Coach Rupp. Popular former players such as Issel and Dampier signed petitions to keep Coach Rupp. It was just a terrible year.

I interviewed Coach Rupp after every game. I never brought up the retirement thing and neither did he. Everybody seemed to recognize it except him. Even at Mississippi State, where they had treated him terribly for years, he got a huge standing ovation. Everybody in the league wanted to do something for him, but they couldn't because he wouldn't admit he was going to retire. Even at the last home game that season, against Auburn, they brought a lot of the All-American players back, but the word retirement was never mentioned. It was a very emotional night.

After beating Auburn, 102-67, the team still had one game left at Tennessee. The Vols had already clinched at least a tie for the SEC championship, but needed to beat UK to get the NCAA bid. If the Cats won, they would share the championship and get the NCAA trip because of their earlier win over Tennessee in Lexington. Harry Lancaster always thought that Adolph was one of those people born under a lucky star who always have good things happen to them, and this game in Knoxville was a good example. Late in the game, Tennessee sent Mike Edwards, a great free-throw shooter, to the line with a one-and-one that could have iced the game. But Edwards blew it and UK held on to win, 67-66. After the game, Coach Rupp told me on the radio show, "They said I'm too old to coach, but I've won more championships than any of 'em and we just won another one, and we're going to the NCAA."

That year's NCAA Mideast Regional was held in Dayton, Ohio, and the Cats surprised everyone by whipping Marquette, 85-69, in the semifinal behind the shooting of Ronnie Lyons. But in the regional final, Florida State, led by former Louisville high school stars Ron King and Otto Petty, exposed UK's lack of quickness and zipped to a 73-54 win. Afterward, Coach Rupp said he might stick around another two or three years. But it was over and everybody knew it.

When UK held a press conference to announce that Joe B. Hall was the new head coach, Coach Rupp didn't bother to attend. The end had come for this great coach and at last he had to accept it.

I had the great pleasure of working with him the last 19 years he coached. I was in my 20s when I began doing Kentucky games and Coach Rupp was a very important person in my life. I admired him tremendously. Many of the things I believe today are things I learned from him.

He was the most superstitious man I've ever known. He always wore a brown suit at the games and one of his monikers was, "The man in the brown suit." When he had his team at a tournament and won the first game, the first thing he did back at his hotel room was wash out his socks. He wasn't taking any chances that a different pair of socks would hurt his cause the next night. He always carried a buckeye, a rabbit's foot and a four-leaf clover in his pocket.

On the day of a game, he searched the grounds for hair pins, and the more he found the better his luck would be that night. On days when Kentucky was faced with a particularly big game, the players were known to salt the grounds around the hotel with hair pins.

He would never break up a starting lineup as long as the team kept winning. Ermal Allen, who was an outstanding basketball and football player for the Wildcats in the early '40s, told me that during the 1939-40 season the team went to Milwaukee to play an excellent Marquette team. They had to stop the train in Cincinnati to take Ermal and a couple of flu-stricken teammates to the hospital. After the team went on to upset Marquette anyway, a recovered Ermal Allen couldn't get his starting job back because the team kept winning. Realizing he had to do something to get back into the lineup, Ermal devised a devious scheme. On the bus from the hotel to the gym at Georgia Tech, Ermal was sitting with Carl "Hoot" Combs, who had taken his job. While Hoot wasn't looking, Ermal took Hoot's basketball shoes and threw them out the window. With Combs shoeless that night, Ermal got his starting job back.

Coach Rupp also detested waiting. When he got on a bus, without ever looking around, he'd say, "Kick 'er doc," and we'd be rolling. Once, at Auburn, the bus left Mike Pratt, and Joe Hall had to go back and get him.

After a trip one time, Coach Rupp asked me if I had a ride home. I told him I had come out in a taxi, so he suggested that I ride with him and that we could go directly from his house to do the TV program. Mrs. Rupp was picking him up and we'd drop her off on the way. Mrs. Rupp was maybe a half hour late and Coach Rupp got more angry by the minute. When she finally arrived, he got in the front seat beside her and I got into the back seat. Coach Rupp lit into her. He ranted and raved about her being late. This went on for 10 or 15 minutes. During that time, Mrs. Rupp hadn't spoken a word. Finally, after deciding she'd heard all she wanted to hear, she turned to him and said, "That's enough, Adolph."

It was like turning off a light switch. He turned to me in the back seat and asked, "Cawood, how did you think we played last night?" He may have been the master of college basketball, but I learned right there who was master of the Rupp household.

We did his TV show live in those days because there was no videotape. There also wasn't any film of the game. The program was actually a half-hour conversation with Adolph. He was a delightful interview and his barbed wit often came through. I recall doing his program with him right after a painful loss when he said this: "We're just not a smart ball club. Not smart at all. When they pass out the Phi Beta Kappa keys this year, I'm afraid there won't be any dangling from our boys' watch chains."

By the time I knew Coach Rupp he was well-heeled. He was also a very frugal man. Harry Lancaster told me that in all the years he had been associated with Adolph, he never knew the man to buy a newspaper. Harry said Coach Rupp would get on a plane and if he saw somebody reading a paper, he would ask if he could see it as soon as that person was finished.

I was telling this story to a group of the media one morning at breakfast in the old Heart of Auburn motel. About the time I finished, Joe Hall walked in and I told him the story I had just related to the group. Joe said, "I just saw him buy one out of the machine outside the motel." Well, I thought, that shoots hell out of Harry's story. Then Joe B. said, "Coach Rupp was standing by the machine as I walked up and he said, 'Joe, have you got any change?' "

That was Coach Rupp for you.

The first time he publicly acknowledged that his coaching career was over was at the basketball banquet at the end of the season. It was a very emotional night. When it came time for the old lion to speak, his voice was quavering. He was close to tears. I can hear those final words as clearly today as I did the night he spoke them. He said, "For those of you who have gone down the glory road with me, my eternal thanks."

I had a lump in my throat as big as a basketball.

Chapter 8

A Peach Of A Season...Finally

*A*fter getting rid of Charlie Bradshaw, UK interviewed some outstanding coaches to be his replacement: Doug Shively, Homer Rice, Frank Kush, to name three. They even talked to Bud Wilkinson, who had done such a great job at Oklahoma, but he wasn't interested in coming out of retirement. Finally, they went to Notre Dame, which then was enjoying a resurgence under Ara Parseghian, and hired the defensive coordinator, John Ray. Harry Lancaster and Bill Matthews had been impressed with John when they interviewed him in South Bend. Ray also impressed the athletics board when he met with them.

Ray was a big bear of a man with a voice you could hear up and down the halls of the Coliseum. He came in and told the fans what they wanted to hear: UK could win right away. Shortly after that, the "I Believe" bumper sticker came out. Looking back, there's no question that he oversold the program and built the expectations to an unrealistic level. The truth was, Bradshaw had left him about as bare a cupboard as you'll ever expect to see.

As part of the new image he was trying to promote, Ray slightly changed the color of the uniforms and made the helmets look suspiciously like Notre Dame's. He also had the locker rooms painted and bummed carpet for the coaches' offices. I'll give him credit... that was the first semblance of class anybody had tried to bring to UK football since Coach Bryant had left. The facilities had been allowed to slip until they were downright shabby. The UK people just hadn't done much of anything.

Absolutely the only bright spot of Ray's first year was a 10-9 upset of Ole Miss and Archie Manning at Stoll Field in the second game of the 1969 season. Come to think of it, that was about the only bright spot of Ray's four years, in which the records were 2-8, 2-9, 3-8 and 3-8. He brought in some pretty good players — Darryl Bishop, Doug Kotar, Joe Federspiel, David Roller, guys like that — but not nearly enough of them.

I remember in the 1971 opener against Clemson, Kotar, who went on to have an outstanding pro career with the New York Giants, returned a kickoff 95 yards for a touchdown the first time he touched the ball as a college player. The Cats won that one, 13-10, but beat only Virginia Tech and Vanderbilt the rest of the way. The Vandy win was actually a gift. With the scored tied 7-7 late in the game, Vandy took a UK punt and seemed content to just run out the clock and settle for the tie. But when the crowd booed a line plunge, Vandy decided to try a pass. That was a dumb play for such good students. Bishop picked off the pass and went all the way for a 14-7 UK win.

The '72 season wasn't any better, and everybody knew

that Ray was in big trouble when Kentucky went into its final game against Tennessee in Knoxville. The Cats were trailing, 14-7, late in the game, but had a first down at the Vols' nine. When quarterback Bernie Scruggs attempted to pitch out, a Tennessee player named Carl Johnson took it in full stride at the 15 and that was it. That was pretty much typical of the Ray era.

After the season, the athletics board voted to fire him. They told Harry Lancaster to call John and tell him he was gone. But they decided it would look better if Ray resigned, so they told Harry to call him again and see if Ray would go along with it. He told them to go to hell, that he would stay fired, and I sort of admired him for that.

Everybody thinks the Ray era was a disaster, and in most ways it was, but I'll give him credit for one thing: Commonwealth Stadium. He went the length and breadth of the state preaching about how poor the facilities were. I think he, more than anyone, convinced Dr. Otis Singletary that the university really needed a new stadium to be competitive. When he left, the stadium had been approved and they were ready to break ground. Ray never got to coach there, but Commonwealth Stadium was a positive part of his legacy. So was Sonny Collins, who Ray had recruited out of Madisonville and who was a freshman on that 1972 team.

Ray had been the third consecutive assistant that UK had hired and, if you'll notice, they haven't hired another one since then to be the head coach. You just never know whether a guy who was a top assistant, as Ray had been at Notre Dame, can carry that over and become equally effective as a head coach. The man finally picked to succeed Ray was Fran Curci, who had been the head coach at the University of Miami in Florida. Today it's sort of difficult to imagine anyone leaving Miami, which was the college game's dominant program of the 1980s and early '90s, to come to UK. But back then, Curci felt the UK job was a definite step up — and he was even a Miami graduate! He just felt that no matter what he did at Miami, people wouldn't come to see them play because of the competition from the Dolphins and all the other outdoor things that people can do year-round in southern Florida.

Dr. Singletary and John Y. Brown Jr., the influential UK alum and Kentucky Fried Chicken magnate, were really the ones who went out and hired Fran. I liked him from day one and became closer to him than I had been to any UK football coach. Fran had a lot of charm, a lot of charisma, and he was very bright. I think his strongest point was that he had a great mental approach toward his players — he could really sell them. He also sold Dr. Singletary on the idea of letting him report directly to the president, by-passing the AD. That was written in his contract.

The Curci era and the Commonwealth Stadium era opened on the same day — Saturday, September 15, 1973. UK took a big early lead over Virginia Tech before a crowd of 44,865, then had to hold off a Gobbler rally for a 31-26 victory. I remember Fran telling me that the team was almost looking for a way to lose, and that he had never experienced that. To this day, that losing attitude is what the UK coaches are trying to overcome.

After a few games, Fran decided to go strictly with the Veer offense, an option attack that was popular at the time, because he had an excellent running quarterback in Mike Fanuzzi and a terrific tailback in Collins. He looked pretty smart when the Cats went down to Jackson, Miss., in their fourth game and whipped a good Mississippi State team, 42-14. Fanuzzi called all the plays at the line in that game, and most of the time he called Collins' number, which is why Sonny wound up with 229 yards and four touchdowns. The team finished with a 5-6 record, a major improvement for UK, and nobody blew them out. They even took a winning record into their last two games, but lost both by two points — 20-18 to Florida at Gainesville and 16-14 to Tennessee in Lexington.

The 1974 team went 6-5, UK's first winning season since 1965. Once again, Fanuzzi and Collins were formidable weapons in the Veer. A couple of victories — 20-13 over LSU and 40-24 over Florida, both in Commonwealth — gave the fans reason to hope that UK was finally on the brink of becoming competitive in the SEC. But then, just when it seemed as if UK was ready to get over the hump, it all came unraveled in 1975 when the Cats dropped to 2-8-1 in what turned out to be an unhappy senior season for

135

Collins, the school's all-time leading rusher.

It started with a 15-9 loss to Auburn on the night of Saturday, October 9. Leading 9-0 with less than seven minutes to play, Kentucky gave up two quick Auburn TDs after Collins and Steve Campassi fumbled away kickoffs. A few days later, a disc jockey went on the air in Lexington and suggested that some point-shaving was involved. That turned out to be completely irresponsible — a guy would get fired on the spot for that today — but it really got the rumor mill churning. The FBI even came in to investigate.

Later that season, Elmore Stephens, a former UK player, and a former student manager were mentioned in connection with the murder of a guy named Leron Taylor. Since Collins and Stephens had been good friends, Collins was implicated in the thing and interrogated vigorously. That was really on his mind, even though he had nothing to do with it, as it turned out.

Nevertheless, with all these distractions, the team just came unglued. I don't think there's anything Curci could have done to keep it together under those bizarre circumstances.

In '76, however, the Wildcats made a big turnaround. Curci had brought in some really good players from out of state: Derrick Ramsey and Art Still from New Jersey, Jim Kovach and Mike Siganos from Ohio, to name a few. They jelled in '76 and used a 22-6 win over powerful Penn State in Lexington as the springboard to an 8-3 regular season, the school's best record since 1953.

After capping it with a 7-0 win over Tennessee in Knoxville, the team was asked to make a strange decision. The NCAA investigators had come in because of the previous season's problems and had uncovered some rules violations. As a result of that, the NCAA gave UK a choice: The Wildcats could either accept the Peach Bowl bid that was offered them after the Tennessee game and begin their probation after that, or else they could begin their probation immediately and pass up the Peach Bowl for a chance at another bowl bid the following season. Well, Kentucky took the old bird-in-the-hand approach and accepted the Peach Bowl bid. I would have done the same thing.

It turned out to be a great thing for the Peach Bowl, which had its first sold-out game ever, including an incredible 37,000 Kentuckians who followed the team to Atlanta to see the Cats play North Carolina. Since the Peach Bowl had its own radio network, I didn't do the play-by-play of that game, but I did work the sidelines at the network's request. It was the only time in my career that I ever did that, and it came on a day that was extremely cold. Boy, did I miss the warmth of the booth that day!

The score was 0-0 at halftime, but Kentucky and tailback Rod Stewart got it cranked up in the second half. In their first bowl game since the Bryant era, the Cats won, 21-0, giving all those fans plenty of reason to whoop it up that night in Atlanta's fine restaurants and bars. I don't know how much Kentucky money was left in Atlanta that weekend, but it had to have been a bunch.

Although most of that team returned for the 1977 season, nobody expected the Cats to be as good as they were. With Ramsey at quarterback and Still anchoring the defense from his end spot, they got off to a modest start, beating North Carolina, 10-7, in a Lexington rematch of the Peach Bowl. They then went to Baylor and not only got beat, 10-9, but lost Stewart for the season with an injury. As things turned out, that was the only time that team lost. They won their last eight for a final 10-1 record that put them as high as sixth in the national polls.

The pivotal win was over Penn State, 24-20, on October 1 in State College, Pa. Joe Paterno's Nittany Lions were ranked fourth in the country at the time. They had a fine quarterback in Chuck Fusina and a top-notch tailback in Jimmy Cefalo. After spotting Penn State a 9-0 lead, the Cats got back into it when Dallas Owens intercepted a pass and returned it for a TD. After that, the UK defense really shut down Penn State and the offense was more than adequate. That win gave the players the feeling that they were as good as anybody in the country — and, as it turned out, they were.

They went to Georgia on October 22 and put a 33-0 whipping on the Bulldogs. That was the game when Prince Charles of Great Britain, who was in Athens as part of his American visit, reviewed the players, military fashion, on both teams before the game. When he got to the 6'7" Still, he stopped and said, "My, you're a tall one."

He was also a good one. Still made first-team All-American and went on to an all-pro career with the Kansas City Chiefs.

In the next-to-last-game of the season, UK squeezed out a 14-7 win over Florida in Gainesville, but it was a dear one. I've never seen a team get beat up as badly in one game as UK did that day. I mean, when they got off the plane in Lexington, they looked like patients in a M*A*S*H unit returning from a war zone. Ramsey's shoulder was banged up so bad that Curci didn't even bring him out on the field for warmups before the final game against Tennessee in Commonwealth Stadium. He didn't want Tennessee to know until the last moment that Ramsey couldn't even throw it, so Ramsey didn't warm up with the other quarterbacks.

The Vols had a 17-14 lead in the second half when Ramsey finally was forced to throw a pass. He completed it, but he also was in such pain that he grabbed his shoulder and had to leave the game. With UK facing third-and-long, Curci brought in Mike Deaton, who completed a pass to Felix Wilson for 39 yards and a first down. That was the key play in a UK touchdown drive that put the Cats on top, 21-17. The Vols came driving back behind quarterback Jim Streater, but just when it looked shaky for the Cats, Still shook the ball loose on a tackle and Kelly Kirchbaum fell on it to save the win.

After the game, the players gave Curci a victory ride, and then came back on the field to wave to the fans, who stayed around to give them a well-deserved ovation. That was easily the best UK football team of my 39 years. They weren't a fancy team. They just played old-fashioned, smash-mouth football on both sides of the ball. That team proved to me that defense wins games. In fact, the defense was so good all year that the offense knew it didn't have to get a lot of points for the team to win.

At 6'5" and about 210 pounds, Ramsey was more like an old single-wing tailback than a modern quarterback. He wasn't as bad a passer as many thought, but he threw it only to keep the defense honest. He was the team's leading rusher in both '76 and '77, the only times in my 39 years that a quarterback led the team in that department.

With Ramsey at quarterback, the team's motto was, "Here we come, try and see if you can stop us." Almost nobody could.

Chapter 9

The Impossible Job

I can't imagine anything more difficult than succeeding Adolph Rupp as the Kentucky basketball coach. Talk about a tough act to follow — there was no way you could top it and very little chance of even coming close. But Joe B. Hall did remarkably well, even though he always felt the pressure of the great burden. Being a native of Cynthiana who had played for Coach Rupp in the late '40s, Joe knew the program upside down and inside out. That was a blessing, in some ways, but also a curse because Joe knew better than anyone how much basketball meant to people all over Kentucky. But it was a job he really wanted, even though Coach Rupp had made it hard on him.

He got off to a fine start, going 20-8 in 1972-73 with another bunch of "Super Sophs" — Kevin Grevey from Ohio, Jimmy Dan Conner from Kentucky, Mike Flynn from Indiana and Bob Guyette from Illinois. That team got off to a shaky 1-3 start, but came on to win the SEC championship and the trip to Nashville for the NCAA Mideast Regional. UK's first opponent, Austin Peay, was coached by Lake Kelly, who would later become one of Joe's assistants, as would Austin Peay assistant coach Leonard Hamilton. That Austin Peay team was led by Fly Williams, one of the nation's leading scorers, and I remember a clever banner in the Vanderbilt arena that said, "The Fly's open, let's go, Peay."

But Kentucky won a barn-burner, 106-100, to earn a shot at Indiana for the right to advance to the Final Four in St. Louis. Earlier in the season, the Hoosiers had beaten the Cats, 64-58, in Bloomington, and this time they won again, 72-65, behind big Steve Downing. Joe and Indiana coach Bob Knight were good friends then, and I remember Joe saying after the game, "Bobby, I don't think I'm ever going to beat you."

But Knight told him that if they played long enough, it would wind up about 50-50 and, sure enough, that's the way it worked out.

The next season, 1973-74, turned out to be a disaster, the worst of Hall's 13 years. The team got off to a 1-3 start and just never recovered. Grevey, the sensational left-handed junior forward, got hurt and everybody became more and more discouraged as the season wore on. It seemed to me that they let the losing feed on itself instead of fighting as if their lives were at stake. The year was really tough on Joe B. We usually did the pregame show on the afternoon of the game, and many times, after we were through, he would just hang around and talk and talk and talk. He was really low. The team was 12-13 going into its final game, but beat Mississippi State, 108-69, to avoid a losing season.

That summer they went on a 19-game tour of Australia.

The players told me it was the most miserable summer they had ever spent. They played in tiny gyms, traveled on buses with no air conditioning, and sometimes played two or three nights in a row. It was like a cheap barnstorming tour, really, but I think it brought that team much closer together. And it was just in time, too, because there's no doubt that Joe's career was on the line. After that 13-13 year, he couldn't afford another disaster and everybody knew it.

The 1974-75 team got off to a 2-0 start, then went up to play Indiana in Bloomington and absolutely got destroyed. The final score was 98-74, but it could have been much worse had Bobby not called off the dogs. It was just a devastating loss. Late in the game, when the scrubs were playing, Bobby got up to yell at the officials and that kind of got to Joe. He stood up and said something like, "Way to go, Bob," or something sarcastic like that, and Bobby cuffed him on the back of the head. I think Bobby meant to be playful, but it didn't come off that way to Joe or the Kentucky fans. It was sort of like adding insult to injury, and Bobby and Joe, who had been fishing buddies, were never close after that. After that game, as Ralph Hacker and I were riding home, I told him I thought it was going to be a long winter in Lexington.

The next game was against North Carolina in Freedom Hall, and when Kentucky fell behind, 31-16, Joe was so frustrated that he took off his coat and threw it down. I told him later that if he was going to do that every game, I wanted to reserve the back of his shirt for an ad for our postgame show.

But Jimmy Dan Conner took charge at that point and had a great night, scoring 29 as the Cats came back to beat Carolina, 90-78, in what proved to be a crucial game for that team's confidence. After going back to Lexington to win the UKIT, they came back to Freedom Hall and got two more big wins, beating Kansas and Notre Dame. Suddenly the team that had looked so bad against Indiana was beginning to look pretty decent.

That team started four seniors — Grevey, Conner, Flynn and Guyette — and a freshman — Rick Robey, a 6'11" kid Joe recruited out of Louisiana. Everybody had a role: Grevey was the shooter, Conner the leader, Flynn the defensive ace and Guyette the rebounder. Robey, who still had some baby fat on him, added some size and mobility around the basket. That team also had three other freshmen — Jack Givens, Mike Phillips and James Lee — who made important contributions off the bench. Givens, from Bryan Station, and Lee, from Henry Clay, were UK's best recruits out of Lexington since Billy Ray Lickert in the late 1950s.

That '74-75 team turned out to be a darned good one. After the debacle at Indiana, the Wildcats only lost three more games, all in the league, and wound up as SEC co-champions with C.M. Newton's fine Alabama team, even though they had defeated 'Bama twice during the season. As it turned out, both got to go to the NCAA Tournament because that was the year when the field was expanded. After an easy win over Marquette in the first round, the Cats advanced to the Mideast Regional in Dayton, where they beat Central Michigan, 90-73, to set up the game everybody had been wanting since December — a rematch with Indiana.

Going into that game, Knight's team was 31-0 and ranked No. 1 in all the polls. However, Indiana's best scorer, forward Scott May, had suffered a broken arm late in the season and was doubtful, at best, for the UK game. Yet when they announced the starting lineups, here was May, with a cast on his injured arm. Knight later said that starting May had been a psychological mistake because it sent the message that Indiana was worried and desperate. As it turned out, May wasn't much of a factor in what developed into one of the greatest games anybody ever saw. It was close all the way, Kentucky leading for a while and then Indiana leading for a while. Indiana's center, Kent Benson, who had just worn Robey out in the December game, was magnificent again, but this time so were the Cats, especially Flynn, the Hoosier native who was a perfect six-for-six from the floor in the second half.

Near the end, with Kentucky leading, 92-90, the Cats lined up single file right in front of our broadcast spot for an inbounds play and I caught Grevey's eye. He just sort of wearily raised his eyebrows and went, "Phew!" as if to indicate what a tense, tough game it had been. Moments later it was over, with UK winning by that 92-90 score.

I think, even now, Joe B. would say that was the greatest win of his career, just as Knight would say it was his most bitter loss. It was more than just a win that ruined Indiana's unbeaten season and gave Hall his first trip to the Final Four; it avenged that humiliating loss in December and established Joe B. as a coach.

I drove behind the team bus on the way back to Lexington, and I'll never forget what happened after we crossed the Ohio River into Kentucky. The state police picked us up at that point and escorted us all the way home. At just about every overpass, fans were waiting to cheer and show the homemade banners they had made. It was just incredible. And then there was a big celebration at the Coliseum when the team got back to Lexington. The only problem with this, in looking back, is that it made the Final Four trip to San Diego almost anti-climactic. All the emotion had been spent in that win over Indiana.

On Final Four Saturday, there was a lot of speculation about a championship game between Louisville, which was playing UCLA, and Kentucky, which was meeting Syracuse. Well, the Cats handled Syracuse fairly easily, 95-79, but the Cards lost a great one to UCLA in overtime. Louisville had a great chance to win in regulation, but Terry Howard, a senior guard who had been 28-for-28 at the free throw line during the season, missed his first one, enabling UCLA to tie it and take it into overtime.

After that win, UCLA's John Wooden pulled a real slick one, announcing at his press conference that he would retire after Monday night's championship game. Immediately, everybody began speculating about his successor. Joe B. had the best line: "It should be me," he said. "Why ruin two lives?"

The coach who had followed Rupp understood better than anyone how tough it would be for the coach who followed Wooden. Everybody assumed that U of L coach Denny Crum, who had played and coached under Wooden at UCLA, would jump at the chance, but Crum held a press conference on Sunday to take himself out of it. (The job eventually went to Gene Bartow, then at Memphis State.)

If Kentucky was emotionally flat because of the Indiana game, UCLA became equally fired up because of Wooden's announcement. I'll always think that was the difference in the 1975 championship game, which the Bruins won, 92-85, to give Wooden his 10th title in 12 years. I thought Wooden really took advantage of the situation and got away with murder that game. Several times he was out on the floor, stomping his foot, but the officials weren't about to call a "T" on him in his final game.

At the same time, Kentucky just didn't play well, hitting only 38 percent from the field. Only Grevey, who closed his fine career with 34 points, played anywhere close to his normal game. Still, there was another huge celebration when the team got back to Lexington. It was a great season and a great coaching job by Joe B., who finally got the monkey off his back.

The 1975-76 team got off to a sluggish start, which might have been expected for a team with one junior (Larry Johnson) and four sophomores (Robey, Givens, Phillips and Lee) in its starting lineup. Amazingly, however, they came within a whisker of upsetting Indiana in Freedom Hall. With only seconds to go, Kentucky was ahead by two and had the ball, but Johnson took an ill-advised shot — he should have waited to be fouled — and Indiana got the rebound.

Everybody knew that May would shoot, which he did, but he missed. But somehow Benson, who was staggering and sort of falling down, swatted the rebound into the basket to tie it and send it into overtime. The Hoosiers went on to win, 77-68, but that was one of their closest calls in what was to be an unbeaten, national-championship season. They were lucky to beat Kentucky, but you've got to win a couple like that when you go unbeaten.

After a loss to Vanderbilt on Valentine's Day, 1976, the team was only 10-10 and, with Robey out with a knee injury, it looked as if the rest of the year would be a struggle at best. But they won their next five to take a 15-10 record into the last home game, a March 8 contest against Mississippi State, which also was to be the last UK game in Memorial Coliseum. With only a minute and a half to go, the Cats were down by seven and I said on the air, "It's over, they're not going to leave Memorial Coliseum on a winning

152

note."

Besides being without Robey, they also had lost Phillips, who had been kicked out, and Lee, who had fouled out. The Mississippi State players were so confident that during a timeout, instead of huddling, some of them went over to talk to their play-by-play man on the radio. But doggone if Kentucky didn't come back to tie it in regulation and then win it, 94-93, in overtime.

It was just one of those impossible wins, but then, Kentucky usually found magic when it played in the Coliseum. It was just a great place to watch basketball, and the crowds made it just about the most intimidating place anywhere. The students used to line up outside two days before a big game and sleep on the sidewalk to get tickets. Somehow — and I never did figure this out — the football players not only always got in, but managed to get seats right next to the band. The football players really supported the basketball team and had a big role in making the Coliseum so loud and intimidating that even good players tended to play poorly on their first visit.

After that Mississippi State game, the Cats accepted a bid to play in the NIT in New York's Madison Square Garden — their first appearance there since some of Rupp's best players had been implicated in the point-shaving scandals that erupted there in the early 1950s. Thanks largely to Hall, whom I thought put on a coaching clinic, the Cats beat Niagara, Kansas State, Providence and North Carolina-

Charlotte to win the title. The 71-67 win over Charlotte, which was coached by former Lexingtonian Lee Rose and led by Cedric "Cornbread" Maxwell, meant that the team had won its last 10 in a row for a final 20-10 record, a heckuva finish that gave the players a lot of confidence.

The Cats moved into Rupp Arena for the 1976-77 season, and officially dedicated the huge new place on November 27, 1976, with a 72-64 win over Wisconsin. They brought Coach Rupp back that night and had a long standing ovation for him before the game. Later, when they played Kansas, Coach Rupp's alma mater, they presented him with a big easy chair that would be his seat at home games. Kansas presented him with a plaque. I thought it was nice to see Coach Rupp getting that kind of recognition, considering how he wouldn't let them do anything during his last season.

That team turned out to be a very good one, going 24-3 during the regular season. They absolutely crushed a good Notre Dame team that was ranked No. 1 at the time, 102-78, in Freedom Hall, and South Carolina coach Frank McGuire, after watching his team suffer a 98-67 trouncing, said it was the best Kentucky team he had seen since the Fabulous Five. Of their three regular-season defeats, two came to Tennessee, which had a pair of All-Americans in Bernard King and Ernie Grunfeld. When the Vols came to Lexington, the fans were still angry with Grunfeld, who had pulled a fast one the previous year by substituting himself for a teammate for a couple of crucial free throws. One of the banners in Rupp Arena said, "Ernie Grunfeld...A True Volunteer." Still, Tennessee won, 71-67, in overtime, and later added an 81-79 win in Knoxville.

In the NCAA Tournament, the Cats had a couple of easy wins over Princeton and VMI before losing, 79-72, to North Carolina in the East Regional championship game. That was when Dean Smith was running his "Four Corners" delay game so well with Phil Ford as his main ball handler. After getting the lead, the Tar Heels just spread it out and Kentucky could never catch up. At one point, Smith called Rick Robey an S-O-B because he thought Robey was playing too rough. Kentucky fans no doubt thought the same about Smith for his Cats-and-mouse game. There's no question in my mind that Dean Smith is responsible for the 45-second clock. Fans just got tired of watching great athletes being made to stand around and hold the ball. And one more thing: As great a coach as Dean is, he didn't invent the so-called "Four Corners." Babe McCarthy had run it years before at Mississippi State, except he called it "The Domino."

Heading into the 1977-78 season, Kyle Macy, who had transferred from Purdue, became eligible, and he was to prove to be the ingredient that elevated a very good team into a national championship outfit. Macy's dad was a high school coach, and he had taught Kyle to be a coach on the floor. He was a very smart player who almost never made a mental error, in addition to being an outstanding shooter

155

(both from the field and the foul line) and an excellent passer. With Kyle running the show, all the other roles fell into
place: Robey and Phillips were the "Twin Towers" around
the basket, Givens was the scorer with that soft, left-handed
jumper of his, Truman Claytor was the zone-buster, and Lee
became the "Super Sub" off the bench. It was a team with
no weaknesses, a team that could pound you to death inside
or kill you softly with jumpers from the perimeter, and that's
why it was ranked No. 1 from Day One.

After they had drilled the Soviet National team in an
exhibition, the Russian coach said, "Best team I ever look."
His English might not have been perfect, but everybody in
college basketball got his message.

Even so, everybody already was feeling the pressure. At
one point during the preseason, Lee balked when Hall
ordered him to do some running and even quit for a couple of
days. Hall let him back before the press could get wind of it.

On December 10, while the team was earning a tough 73-
66 win at Kansas, Coach Rupp died in a Lexington hospital. It
was ironic that he passed away the very night the Cats were
playing his alma mater. His death wasn't surprising, however.
Since the summer, it had been apparent to just about everybody that Rupp was fighting a losing battle against cancer.
After he was put into the hospital for the last time, Harry
Lancaster went to see him. "I've kinda been looking for you,"
Coach Rupp said, and then they made their peace after all
those bitter years of not speaking to each other.

After the Kansas game that night, I went back to the Holiday Inn and my friend Jim Payne said, "Come on down to the room and let's have a drink." When I got there, I noticed everybody was very quiet. Seth Hancock was on the phone with somebody back in Kentucky. It was then that Jim told me, "Coach Rupp is dead." I never did have that drink. I just went back to my room feeling a great sadness that this great man was gone.

Back in Lexington, many of his former players, the boys who had taken him down what he called "the glory road," attended his huge funeral. Ralph Beard, one of the players who had been involved in the point-shaving scandal, was there. Coach Rupp held a grudge against them for many years, but he finally had forgiven them. After the funeral, the procession drove past the Coliseum, where it slowed for a few moments, and then past Rupp Arena, where it slowed again, on the way to the cemetery.

Whenever I think about Coach Rupp, I'll always remember something Whack Hyder, the old Georgia Tech coach, said. "Everybody in the South should pay tribute to Adolph Rupp," Hyder said, "because he made basketball in the South."

Coach Rupp would have loved those 1977-78 Cats and the way Joe Hall handled them. They won 14 in a row before losing to Alabama, then won three more before encountering their first crisis. In Baton Rouge, they dropped a 95-94 overtime game to the same LSU team they had waxed by 20 at home earlier in the season. Well, not exactly the same LSU team. The Tigers managed to win despite the fact that all five starters had fouled out. LSU's coach Dale Brown, who had charged after the game in Rupp Arena that Kentucky was "brutalizing" the game, was as ecstatic as Hall was angry.

On the postgame show, Hall told me this team's nickname should be the "Folding Five." He was about as hot as I had ever seen him, and he hadn't cooled off by the time we got to Ole Miss for the next game. On the way to practice, he slammed the bus door shut right in the face of a couple of dawdling players and made them take cabs to the arena. Then, during the game, he was a wild man, substituting every time a player made the least little mistake. They won, 64-52, which was almost a miracle under the circumstances, but the players got the message. They played better after that, and closed out the regular season with a 25-2 record.

The next crisis came in their first NCAA Tournament game against Florida State in Knoxville. The Seminoles had a 39-32 halftime lead, which caused Joe B. to do a very courageous thing — at least it looks courageous in retrospect. At the time it looked foolhardy because had it backfired, Hall might have lost his job. What he did was put three substitutes — Fred Cowan, Dwane Casey and LaVon Williams — in the starting lineup for the second half. They closed the gap by only two points, but they also got Hall's message across.

When Hall went back to his regular starters, they rolled to an 85-76 victory that moved them on to the NCAA Mideast Regional in Dayton. After an easy 91-69 romp past Miami of Ohio, the Cats met Michigan State, led by a precocious freshman named Earvin "Magic" Johnson, for the regional title and the trip to the Final Four.

Nobody had ever seen a 6'9" point guard before, so in the first half Magic sort of mesmerized everybody as State controlled the tempo on offense and fell back into a 3-2 zone on defense. The Spartans had a 27-22 lead at halftime and nobody seemed quite certain what to do. However, just as the Cats were leaving the locker room, Leonard Hamilton, then one of Hall's assistants and his top recruiter, had a brainstorm. He suggested to Joe B. that maybe UK could get some points by having Robey come out high and set picks for Macy, who would either pull up for the jumper or try to draw fouls while driving. In addition, Hall decided to junk UK's man-to-man in favor of a 1-3-1 zone trap, in the hope of closing Magic's passing lanes.

It all worked beautifully. With Macy hitting 10 straight free throws down the stretch, the Cats won, 52-49, to earn the trip to the Final Four in St. Louis. In my 39 years, I think Macy was the best clutch player the Cats ever had. If I could pick any UK player I covered to take the final shot in a game, Macy would be the guy.

In the semifinals, Kentucky met an outstanding Arkansas team featuring the "Triplets" (Sidney Moncrief,

Ron Brewer and Marvin Delph) and coached by Eddie Sutton, who UK fans would get to know better in later years. The Wildcats won, 64-59, but not without a struggle. In fact, the players told me later that Arkansas was the best team they played all year. Yet Kentucky's inside power eventually proved to be too much for Arkansas' quickness, so UK moved into the title game for the second time in four years, this time against a talented but young Duke team coached by Bill Foster.

At the Sunday press conferences, the Cats suffered one of their worst beatings of the season. Not by any team, but by the national media. The UK players were tabbed as being grim and serious. Duke was happy and carefree. The contrast was so striking that the columnists had a field day with it. Kentucky got all the worst of it, and I thought that was grossly unfair. Sure, they were serious, but who wouldn't be? It's tough to be No. 1 every day of the season. A lot of teams, in fact, have just buckled under the pressure. But instead of being given credit for the way they handled it, the UK players were criticized because they weren't as frisky as the young Duke players.

After the press conference, the rumor sprang up that Hall was going to quit after the championship game. However, when the writers nailed him down before UK's practice, he laughed and denied it.

The players went into the game confident they were better than Duke, which is one of the reasons why they played one of their best games. There was a hole in the middle of Duke's zone, created by the fact that they had to honor the big guys underneath while still guarding Macy and Claytor on the perimeter. Well, Goose Givens filled it perfectly, getting loose for 41 points in UK's 94-88 victory. He was so hot that he even hit the edge of the backboard with a shot from the corner, but still made it. Jack could have scored even more, except that Hall pulled the starters when he thought the victory was locked up. He had to quickly put them back in after Duke made a little run, but Lee brought the game — and the season — to a perfect ending with a thunderous dunk. Finally, the players were able to smile and celebrate.

In the locker room, I asked Joe B. if I could get a seat on the team plane and he told me to see Cecil Dunn, the Lexington attorney who was his good friend and sort of unofficial traveling secretary on the road. Cecil found a seat for me, but we had to hang around the St. Louis airport a long time waiting for the plane. When we finally got to Blue Grass Field, it was about 3 a.m., but there still was a wild crowd of about 10,000 waiting to see the team. The airport was a mess, just a wreck, but they brought the team in through a side door and took the players up to a balcony, where everyone was introduced and cheered. It was a night that had been a long time coming. Kentucky finally was back on top of the basketball world.

Chapter 10

The Dream Game And
The Nightmare In Seattle

*I*n the fall of 1978, Jim Host, who owned the UK radio rights, began talking to me about leaving WHAS, moving to Lexington, and forming my own company in partnership with him. Back in those days, Jim was making all the trips and, since we both are early risers, we had a lot of coffee-shop conversations before anybody else showed up. We talked and talked. He offered to put up the money to get it started, and I would take a larger salary than I was making at WHAS.

I didn't know what to do. I was happy and comfortable at WHAS, and Frances, who I'd married in 1974 after a long courtship, was the business manager there. Frances and I wrote down the pluses and minuses, and went over the list, point by point. Finally, we decided to give it a shot.

I took my letter of resignation to Bob Morse, who was then the acting station manager, in January 1979. He thought it took a lot of guts to make that kind of move at age 52. After we talked, he came back to my office downstairs and said, "Are you sure? Is there some reason you haven't told me about?"

When I assured him there wasn't, he asked if I'd continue to do commentaries for WHAS and work for them during

Kentucky Derby week. I said sure, and I did those things until I retired. Barry Bingham Jr. couldn't have been nicer. He sent me a memo that began, "You old snake..." But he told me that if things didn't work out with Host, I could always come back, and that meant a lot more to me than the VCR and the other nice going-away gifts they gave us. The Binghams were great to me, and I'll always have a special place in my heart for them.

So we moved to Lexington and I opened my office February 4, 1979. Maybe a week after I started, I hired Joanne Keenan and we really built this little company together. I lost $31,000 the first year, but we've paid a dividend every year since. It turned out to be the right thing to do, just as Host had promised, but it's just tough to leave a place where you're happy and where you're proud to work.

Once I got all this squared away, I was able to concentrate on the end of what had been a rebuilding season for the basketball program. Of the six most important players on the '78 NCAA championship team, the only ones returning were the starting guards, Kyle Macy and Truman Claytor. But as the season wore on, the crowds began to get excited about a 6'3" freshman from Dayton named Dwight Anderson. I nicknamed him "The Blur" because he was the quickest player I'd ever seen in a UK uniform. Still is, for that matter. In the third game of the season, against Kansas in Rupp Arena, he gave the fans their first glimpse of the way he could change a game. With 16 seconds to go in overtime, the Cats trailed Kansas, 66-60. A hopeless situation, right? Well, Anderson came in after Claytor fouled out. He hit a field goal and two free throws to cut it to two. Then, with time almost gone, he made this incredible leap out of bounds for a loose ball that he somehow knocked back to Macy, who hit the jumper to tie it. Kansas' best player, Darnell Valentine, in what was a purely reflex move, called a timeout. But because the Jayhawks didn't have any left, they were hit with a technical foul, and Macy, old "Mr. Clutch," hit the free throw to win it, 67-66.

At the end of December, Anderson made a splash on national TV against Notre Dame in Freedom Hall. The Irish had gone to a triangle-and-two defense to keep Macy and Claytor from killing them from outside. But Joe B. put Anderson inside the zone, even though he was a guard, and Notre Dame couldn't handle his quickness. After UK's 81-76 win, Al McGuire, who was in his first year as an NBC analyst, raved about Anderson. I guess you could say a star was born, because McGuire seemed to mention Anderson every chance he got the rest of the season. I guess I should feel lucky that Al didn't take credit for being the first to call Anderson "The Blur."

Even with Macy, Anderson and Claytor, that team struggled because of its weak inside game — Cowans and Williams were the best inside players — and took only a 16-10 record into the SEC Tournament, which was being renewed for the first time since 1952. The event was held in

Birmingham, and I remember it mostly for the great way Macy and Claytor played. After getting past Ole Miss in their first game, the Cats played a fine Alabama team, led by Reggie "Mule" King, and the result was a barn-burner that many still think may be the best game ever played in the tournament. UK finally won, 101-100, to earn the right to play LSU, the league regular-season champion, in the semifinals.

It looked bad for the Cats when Anderson injured his ankle 23 seconds into the game and was lost for the rest of the season. Incredibly, however, Macy and Claytor, who may have been the two best players in the conference, picked up the slack and led UK to an 80-67 win.

In the championship game against Tennessee, it was obvious that UK was a tired team. The Cats still played their hearts out, considering it was their fourth game in four nights, but they finally lost, 75-69, in overtime. Their 19-11 record earned them a berth in the NIT and a first-round game at home against Clemson. But they were still a tired-looking team and lost again, 68-67, to end the season.

Knowing they needed to replenish their talent supply, Hall and his staff worked especially hard on recruiting during that '79-80 season. They went right down to the wire with Virginia for 7'4" Ralph Sampson, the top prospect in the country, and they thought they had him. In fact, the night Sampson was to announce his choice, we had a radio crew in his hometown so we could announce it on the "Big Blue

Line." Joe B. even had a private plane standing by to take him down there. Sampson waited until the last minute before finally picking Virginia. UK fans couldn't be too disappointed, though, because Hall brought in a super class that included 7'1" Sam Bowie, guard Dirk Minniefield of Kentucky state champion Lafayette High, the promising Derrick Hord from Tennessee, and Charles Hurt from Shelby County.

With all those freshmen, the '79-80 team was young, but it also had a couple of veteran senior guards in Macy and Jay Shidler. It lost to Duke, 82-76, in overtime, in the Tipoff Classic in Springfield, Mass., then went to play in the Great Alaska Shootout, which it won over Bradley, Alaska and Iona. When we got back and got ready to go on the radio with our Big Blue Line, I told Joe B. that I bet we'd get a recruiting question instead of a question about the Alaska trip or how the freshmen were coming along. Sure enough, the third question was about recruiting. That's never changed.

With Macy running the show and Bowie looking like UK's best seven-footer since Bill Spivey in the early 1950s, that team turned into a pretty good one. In fact, even though Anderson quit the team and transferred to Southern Cal after Hall caught him breaking a team rule in December, it took a 26-4 record into its final regular-season game against LSU in Baton Rouge. With the score tied, 74-74, in overtime, Joe B. called timeout and set up a play for Bowie, mainly because Macy had really been struggling from the field in that game. But they couldn't get it to Sam, so Macy took the jumper and it hit nothing but net. That's the kind of player he was.

LSU came back to upset the Cats, 80-78, in the SEC Tournament, but the team got back on track in the NCAA, beating Florida State, 97-78, in its first-round game in Bowling Green to earn a rematch with Duke in the NCAA Mideast Regional semifinals in Rupp Arena. Once again Duke's experience made the difference — the Blue Devils still had 6-11 Mike Gminski and some others who had played against UK in the '78 championship game — and Macy's career ended with a disappointing 55-54 loss. Even so, Kyle had a great senior year, averaging 15.4 points, and he walked off the floor secure in the knowledge that he would be remembered as one of the most popular players ever to play at Kentucky.

The following week, Louisville beat Iowa and UCLA in the Final Four to win its first NCAA title, and that's when my friend Billy Reed, then sports editor of *The Courier-Journal*, and other members of the media began demanding a regular-season series between UK and U of L. But Joe B. wouldn't hear of it. Like Coach Rupp, he believed UK had nothing to gain by playing other state schools during the regular season. But it was becoming increasingly difficult to ignore Louisville, which had made three Final Four trips since Denny Crum came aboard in 1972.

With Minniefield replacing Macy at point guard in 1980-81, and Bowie emerging as a real force in the middle, the Cats rolled to a 22-4 record in the regular season, only to have a perplexing letdown in the post-season. First Vanderbilt, a team they had drubbed by 14 and 32, upset them, 60-55, in their first game in the SEC Tournament. Then 10 days later, they were upset again, this time by Alabama-Birmingham, 69-62, in the NCAA Mideast Regional in Tuscaloosa. For a team that had been ranked No. 1 in some of the pre-season polls, this was a disappointing way to end the season, and it didn't boost anyone's spirits when Indiana, which UK had beaten, 68-66, in Bloomington in December, won the national title in Philadelphia.

The Cats were expecting to bounce back in a big way in 1981-82, but Bowie suffered a stress fracture in his left shin during pre-season workouts and was declared out for the season. The team was lucky that it had 6'11" sophomore Melvin Turpin, from Lexington Bryan Station High, waiting to replace Bowie. The team took a respectable 20-5 record into the final game of the regular season, only to go into another mysterious tailspin. First came a 94-78 loss to LSU in Baton Rouge. Then, after winning two games in the SEC Tournament, came a 48-46 upset at the hands of Alabama. And most humiliating of all, there was an embarrassing 50-44 loss to Middle Tennessee, a huge underdog, in the NCAA Mideast Regional in Nashville.

Had UK won that game, the Cats would have played
Louisville in the next round. The media were already looking forward to that and so, I think, were the UK players,
which caused them to take Middle Tennessee too lightly. I
also remember Joe B. taking some heat in the media —
unfairly, I thought — for putting so much pressure on his
players during the season that they came up empty at the
end.

Everyone was looking for Bowie to come back in 1982-
83, but the stress fracture was so slow in healing that Sam
underwent bone-graft surgery on October 20, 1982, knock-
ing him out for yet another season. Still, with all five starters
back from the previous season, the Cats took a 21-5 record
into their final game against LSU in Baton Rouge. However,
a 74-60 loss to the Tigers, followed by another quick exit
from the SEC Tournament (a 69-64 loss to Alabama) had a
lot of people wondering if they were ready to do another
fold-up in the NCAA Tournament. But they righted themselves with a 57-40 win over Ohio U. in Tampa that earned
them a spot in the Mideast Regional in Knoxville opposite
Indiana. The other semifinal matched U of L and Eddie
Sutton's Arkansas Razorbacks, meaning that wins by the
Cats and the Cards would finally produce the "Dream
Game," as the newspaper guys were calling it.

After Kentucky had done its part of the job, eliminating
Indiana, 64-59, Joe B. sat at the press table and watched
most of the Arkansas-Louisville game. The Razorbacks had

a big lead in the second half, but Louisville staged a furious comeback and finally won it, 65-63, on a great tip-in by Scooter McCray at the buzzer. Finally, after not playing for 25 years, Kentucky and Louisville would meet. The excitement over the game was so high that it was almost incidental that a Final Four berth in Albuquerque was also at stake.

For a detached observer — and there weren't many of those in Knoxville's Stokely Center that Saturday afternoon — it was a heckuva contest. Playing one of its best games of the season, Kentucky dominated the early play and even took a seven-point lead, 37-30, at halftime. But Louisville went on a 20-8 tear in the second half, turning a 45-38 deficit into a 58-53 lead. UK took those punches and fought right back, however, pulling into a 60-60 tie and then getting possession when a Milt Wagner pass bounced off Lancaster Gordon's shin. After the Cats worked the clock down from 2:24 to 0:16, Minniefield went blowing down the baseline for a layup, only to have Charles Jones tip it into Scooter McCray's hands. When the Cards took a 62-60 lead on Gordon's short jumper, Hall called time with eight seconds left. During the timeout, Hall sent in Jim Master for a three-guard alignment that confused the Cards long enough for Master to knock down a 12-footer just before the buzzer to send it into overtime.

Later, some UK fans couldn't help but wish that Master had missed the shot, because after Jones outjumped Turpin for the opening tip in overtime, the Cards used their quickness for an 8-0 run that sealed their 80-68 win. In outscoring UK 18-6, the Cards made all six of their shots from the field and all six free throws. I thought it was just a matter of the better team finally proving itself.

I wasn't surprised when the UK athletics board, overruling objections by Hall and athletics director Cliff Hagan, ordered Hagan to enter into negotiations with U of L for a regular-season series. John Y. Brown, who was then the governor, was in favor of it. So were a lot of people high up in the administration. In the press room before the game in Knoxville, Bill Sturgill, one of Dr. Singletary's closest friends and a very powerful member of UK's Board of Trustees, told me he thought the time had come.

Coach Rupp had believed that by playing other teams in the Commonwealth, UK had everything to lose and nothing to gain. His reasoning was that from border to border, none of the other schools enjoyed the tremendous popularity Kentucky had. He felt by playing those schools it could hurt Kentucky's recruiting by elevating the stature of the other teams. He also felt that Kentucky might lose fan support in the areas where those schools were located.

I think Joe B. shared the same feeling. I know he was dead-set against playing Louisville. I have to admit that at the time, I agreed totally. Even though Louisville's program had grown tremendously under Denny Crum, I couldn't conceive of one single advantage Kentucky would get out of the series. The future proved me wrong.

As it turned out, UK didn't have to wait long to have another crack at U of L. In fact, the first regular-season game was also UK's home opener of the 1983-84 season, and, with Bowie finally back and healthy, the Cats administered a 65-44 licking to the Cards that got the season off to an exciting start.

I first saw Sam when he was a senior at Lebanon High School in Pennsylvania when his team came to Louisville to play at Freedom Hall. Before the game started, Sam really turned the crowd on during warmups by hitting several shots from long distance. After he came to Kentucky, I thought he was the most graceful big man who had played for the Wildcats in my time. I told friends that Bowie would be the best player in Kentucky's storied history. And I think he would have if he hadn't been nagged so much with serious injuries. I admire the courage he showed by fighting through all that, and I'm pleased he has been able to come back from injuries that would have ended most careers.

With Bowie back, that '83-84 club had much the same kind of personnel as the '78 champions. Bowie and Turpin, both seniors, were the so-called "Twin Towers" around the basket, sophomore Kenny Walker played the Jack Givens role reasonably well, Master was the designated zone-buster and Dicky Beal provided quickness and cleverness at the point. In addition, freshman Winston Bennett, the first blue-chipper UK had gotten out of Louisville since Ted Deeken in the early '60s, was an excellent sixth man.

Until the end, it was almost a perfect ride for Hall and his players. They went 12-0 before dropping back-to-back SEC games on the road to Auburn and Florida. They lost twice more to league opponents in the regular season, but still became the first team to win both the league's season and tournament championships since the tournament was revived in 1979. Going into the NCAA Tournament with a 26-4 record, they trounced Brigham Young in Birmingham to earn the right to play at home in the Mideast Regional, where they faced — surprise! — Louisville again in the semifinal.

After not playing for 25 years, the rivals now were squaring off for the second time in a season. The Cardinals had improved enough to make a game of it, but some late heroics by Beal and Bennett pushed UK to a 72-67 win. Then the Cats earned Hall his third Final Four trip by polishing off Illinois, 54-51, in the regional title game.

Afterward, while Hall and his players were celebrating, Illinois coach Lou "Lou-Do" Henson complained bitterly about the officiating. He made so much of a fuss, in fact, I think that's what led the NCAA to eventually put in the rule that no team could play a tournament game on its home floor.

What happened next was the strangest game of my 39 years. I still can't explain it, and neither can Joe Hall or any of the players. Pitted against tournament favorite Georgetown and its menacing junior center, Patrick Ewing, in the national semifinals in the Seattle Kingdome, the Cats turned in a fine first half and went to the locker room with a surprising seven-point lead. But then came the great UK nightmare. In the second half, the Cats took 33 shots and made only three. It was just an absolute shocker.

Had it happened in the first half, you could maybe say they were intimidated.

But this came after they had played so well for 20 minutes. And the thing was, they were getting good shots. The Hoyas won, 53-40, but nobody could explain such a big fold-up, which was very atypical of Kentucky teams. Unfortunately, that left a sour aftertaste on what had otherwise been a terrific season.

With Bowie, Turpin, Master and Beal gone, everybody knew 1984-85 would be a rebuilding year, but there were still a lot of shocked folks when the team lost four in a row after winning its opener against Toledo. Then, after seeming to right itself with an eight-game winning streak, the team lost four of five conference games that put it at 9-8.

Somewhere in there, I don't exactly remember when, Joe B. first told me he was thinking about quitting. It wasn't so much the team as the fact that *The Courier-Journal* had begun investigating the 323 tickets Hall controlled in Rupp Arena. The *Herald-Leader*, which was a sort of little brother in those days, got into it too, because they were afraid of getting beat on a story in their home territory. *The Courier-Journal* couldn't find out enough to go with much of a story, but the *Herald-Leader* kept digging and eventually switched from tickets to other areas of the program. Anyhow, I think that got to Joe B. a little bit. Whenever he told me he was thinking about getting out, I told him to wait three or four years and we'd retire together.

That team only had a 16-11 record in the regular season, and it lost to Florida in its only SEC Tournament game. Nevertheless, with the NCAA field now expanded to 64 teams, it got a spot in the West Regional and acquitted itself well, beating both Washington and Nevada-Las Vegas to earn a spot opposite St. John's in the West semifinals in Denver. That figured to be the end of the road, because St. John's had a fine team led by All-American Chris Mullin.

The day of the game, Joe B. went on a sort of sentimental journey by taking the team for a practice to Regis College, where he had been given his first college head coaching job. I remember him saying something like, "Wouldn't it be funny if my college career ended where it started?" Later that day one of Joe's buddies came up to me and told me that if the team lost that night, Joe was going to announce his resignation on the post-game show.

Well, the team lost, 86-70, in a game where Kenny Walker got poked in the eye. I don't think they could have beaten St. John's even if that had not happened, but it sure didn't help. After the game, Joe B. refused to say anything about quitting in his post-game press conference, so all the writers followed him out to courtside for the post-game show. CBS, which also had gotten wind of it, brought its cameras over and stayed on the air. Before we started, Joe leaned over and told me he was going to read a statement, but to just go ahead and talk about the game after he was through instead of asking him any questions. Sure enough, he pulled the statement out of his inside jacket pocket and read it. I think it wasn't until the last minute that he knew which way he was going to go, because I think one side of him wanted very much to stay. He vacillated to the very end.

Looking back, I'd have to say that Joe B. Hall did one helluva job. In 13 years, he won eight conference championships, one NCAA championship and one NIT title at a time when the NIT still meant something. In addition, he took two other teams to the Final Four. That's an incredible record that may not be matched again, and the fact that he did it while following Coach Rupp made it even more remarkable. As the years have passed, I think Joe's record looks better and better.

Chapter 11

Mr. Clean Comes Home

A couple of things were involved in the downfall of Fran Curci as the UK football coach. One was his growing belief that in order to get the kind of players necessary to be competitive in the SEC, he sometimes had to take a chance on the character of certain players, and that backfired on him a few times. Another was that after the NCAA probation, Dr. Singletary told him the next run-in with the NCAA would also mean the end of his job. As a result, Fran went totally the other way in his recruiting. Maybe too far. He stopped getting the kind of players he had on that '77 team and the results showed in the records: 4-6-1 in 1978, 5-6 in '79, 3-8 in '80, and 3-8 again in '81.

In the last game of that '81 season, UK played Tennessee in Commonwealth Stadium, and everybody knew it would be Fran's last game. Before the opening kickoff, he and Tennessee coach John Majors stood at midfield, talking. As they shook hands, Majors wished Curci good luck. Curci told him he wanted just enough luck to kick Tennessee's butt that day, which UK did, 21-10.

That sent Fran out in a blaze of glory, but it wasn't enough to save his job. Dr. Singletary had no choice — the football program was going swiftly downhill — but it also had to hurt him. I don't think he was ever as close to any coach, either in football or basketball, as he was to Fran. Curci was very bitter, even to the point of talking about suing the university, but he eventually just faded away. I was sorry to see him go, even though I knew his program had gotten away from him. He would always go over the game plan with me before a game, and no coach, before or since, has ever done that.

During the hunt for a replacement, the search committee brought in Howard Schnellenberger. He had been an All-American in the 1950s under Collier, and he was in the process of turning Miami of Florida into a perennial national power. He came in, visited with the UK people and talked to the TV/radio people. Then he went back to Florida and turned it down. With Schnellenberger out of the picture, the university eventually turned to Jerry Claiborne, a native of Hopkinsville who had been a star defensive back at UK under Coach Bryant in the late 1940s. As a coach, Jerry had built winners at Virginia Tech and Maryland. The knocks against him were that he was in his mid-50s and that he wasn't very colorful. But he did have the one thing that mattered the most at that time — the image of a Mr. Clean who wouldn't tolerate cheating and who would emphasize academics.

That first season, he bit the bullet and redshirted everybody he could. That 1982 team went 0-10-1, the first time UK ever had a winless season, but Jerry laid the groundwork for the kind of program he wanted.

His next team went 6-4-1, an amazing turnaround, and earned a trip to the Hall of Fame Bowl in Birmingham, where it lost, 20-16, to a West Virginia team led by Jeff Hostetler, the quarterback who would later take the New York Giants to a Super Bowl title.

The Cats followed that with an 8-3 record in 1984, Jerry's best record, and a return trip to the Hall of Fame, where they beat a good Wisconsin team, 20-19. That '84 team won all the close games, and the Wisconsin game was no exception. Late in the game, Wisconsin had a field goal attempt that would have won it, but botched the snap, allowing the Cats to escape with the win.

Although Claiborne had the reputation of being conservative, those two bowl teams had a pretty good passing attack. The quarterback in '83, Randy Jenkins, was a good one, but UK didn't miss a beat when Bill Ransdell, whose father had played for UK in the 1950s, moved in to replace him. They also had an excellent runner and receiver in George Adams, who went on to play for the New York Giants. One of my favorites, however, was Paul Calhoun, one of the best defensive backs and punters that Kentucky ever put on the field in my 39 years. During Calhoun's career, he made a couple of big plays by running out of punt formation. One that I remember came against Mississippi State in 1984, which sparked the Cats to a 17-13 win on the road.

After the '84 season, Kentucky fans were feeling better about the football program than they had in years. Besides the winning records and the bowl trips, Claiborne had taken his broom and swept the program clean. When Curci was in charge, you often were afraid to pick up the paper because there might be another story about a player who had gotten into trouble. But Claiborne ended all that. He recruited good kids who worked hard and went to class.

At the same time, however, Kentucky still wasn't getting enough talent to be more than middle-of-the-pack in the SEC. Even in the 9-3 season, the Cats were only 3-3 in the league, and a couple of the losses — to LSU and Georgia — were blowouts. But Claiborne was the beneficiary of a softer non-conference schedule that had been Curci's idea. When Commonwealth Stadium was built, you see, Harry Lancaster felt that the only way to fill it for non-conference games was to schedule big names like Oklahoma and Penn State. But Curci convinced Harry's successor, Cliff Hagan, that with so many tough league games, UK needed to play non-conference teams it could beat.

After that 9-3 season, Claiborne's teams flirted with .500 the rest of Jerry's career — 5-6 in 1985, 5-5-1 in '86, 5-6 in '87, 5-6 in '88, and 6-5 in '89. It was during the '87 season that I had my second run-in with a coach. During the team's 19-18 loss to Rutgers in Giants' Stadium, Carwell Gardner made a late hit and got a penalty that probably cost UK the game. Ralph Hacker made one of those mistakes that all of us make sooner or later when you're dealing with an open microphone. He said the coaching staff "ought to put Carwell on the bus and send him home."

Although Ralph publicly apologized to Carwell after we got back home, a lot of people were upset by it. Ralph called me that week and said Jerry wanted to meet with us in his office. We both figured it was to talk about Ralph's remarks concerning Gardner. Claiborne seemed very nervous when we got there.

"Both of you were here when I came," he said, "and I know you'll both be here when I leave." He went on to say that his staff and his family were upset and that he thought the three of us should meet to clear the air.

But instead of bringing up the Gardner incident, he mentioned another comment Ralph had made, something about, "Oh, well, we don't have to wait much longer...basketball practice starts on October 15." I knew that I had said nothing to that effect because I had taped the game, as I always do, and had listened to every word of the broadcast. When I next met with Jerry at the WVLK studios to do his Big Blue Line, I handed him the cassette of the game and told him if he could find anything I had said that was unfair, I would apologize. He called me the next morning and said he had listened to the tape and that I had been totally fair. That's the only run-in we ever had.

At the end of the '87 season, UK went into the Tennessee game needing a win for a winning record. They played the Vols tough that afternoon in Commonwealth Stadium and seemed on the brink of victory late in the game. Trailing 24-22, the Cats got a first-and-goal inside the Tennessee five. Then, however, Claiborne sent his best runner, Mark Higgs, into the line four straight times. Each time he came up short, allowing Tennessee to escape with the victory. Boy, the coach's call-in show was flooded with second-guessers after that.

That also was a tough way for Higgs to end his career. He was only a little guy — 5-5 or 5-6 at the most — but, other than Sonny Collins and Rodger Bird, he was the most exciting runner that UK produced during my 39 seasons. I'm not sure how fast he was in straight-ahead speed, but he was elusive and quick and explosive. Every time he touched the ball, he was a threat to go all the way with it, and let's face it, UK just hasn't had many players like that. As a senior in '87, he gained 1,278 yards rushing, averaging 6.6 yards every carry. He also scored 10 touchdowns and had another 233 yards receiving. I thought he was a heckuva football player and, to tell you the truth, I wasn't really surprised when he proved to be a big asset for the Miami Dolphins of the NFL.

With Higgs gone, the Cats opened the 1988 season with a 2-2 record when they played host to Bill Curry's Alabama Crimson Tide. Once again, they seemed to have the game won, only to lose it in bitter fashion, letting the Tide march to the game-winning touchdown on their last possession.

That drive featured a scramble in which Alabama's quarterback turned a fourth-and-long into a first down. Then they connected on a pass on the last play of the game for a 31-27 win. I think that loss, along with the Tennessee game the previous season, might have been the most heartbreaking of Jerry's career at UK. Had the Cats beaten the Tide, I think they could have gone on to win six or seven games and maybe even go to a bowl. Instead, they finished 5-6 for the second consecutive year and there was a lot of grumbling that maybe it was time for a change. I know for a fact that a couple of influential boosters twice went to Jerry — once to ask him to get some new assistants and later to suggest that maybe he should step aside. But both times he wouldn't hear of it.

After the final game of the 1989 season, C.M. Newton, who had been hired to replace Hagan as the athletics director, went to Jerry and asked for a timetable about how much longer he intended to coach. He wasn't dropping any hints or putting any pressure on Jerry. In fact, I'm confident Jerry could have stayed as long as he wanted. But Jerry decided to go ahead and resign. He said it didn't have anything to do with the boos he had gotten at the last home game against Tennessee, although that had to hurt him. It probably had more to do with the fact that recruiting was at hand, and I think Jerry was just tired of that part of it. The university sweetened it for him by agreeing to keep him on the payroll as a fundraiser for the duration of his contract.

I think he left the program in better shape for the new coach than at any time since Collier replaced Bryant. On the field, his teams were competitive, even though he didn't recruit enough of the high-caliber players it takes to win in the SEC. In fact, he didn't even get all the best players from Kentucky, which is a must for any UK coach. But he took good people and made them competitive through hard work. The biggest part of his legacy, though, was that he put the "student" back in the term "student-athlete." His players graduated to the point that UK came to rank among the national leaders in that area. They also stayed out of trouble. I think most people in Kentucky were proud of his accomplishments because no longer did you have to fear picking up the paper and reading about a football player getting into trouble.

One thing I always respected about Jerry was that he had the same set of rules for everybody, stars as well as benchwarmers. He was a straight arrow and a good coach to whom the university always should be grateful.

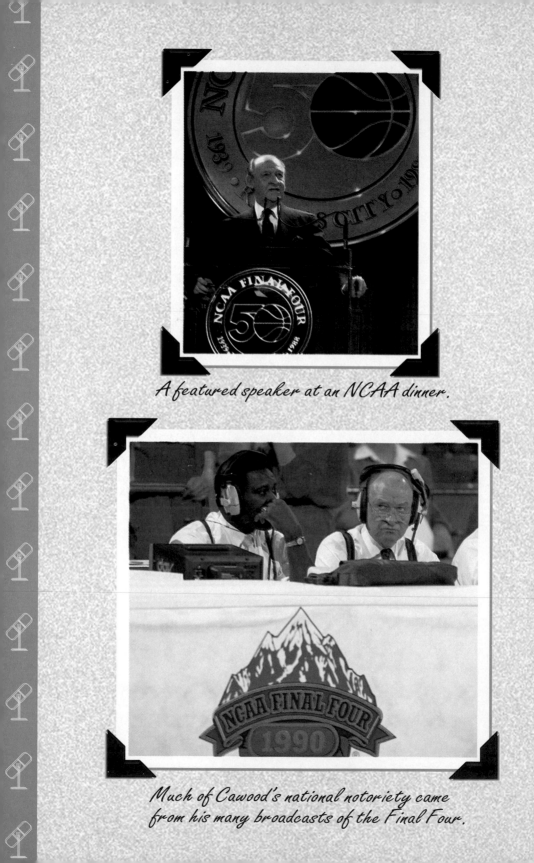

A featured speaker at an NCAA dinner.

Much of Cawood's national notoriety came from his many broadcasts of the Final Four.

With Dick Vitale (above) and signing autographs after a game (right).

Fans came out in droves for a local book-signing of "Cawood's Comments."

Cawood talks horses with trainer D. Wayne Lukas.

Cawood poses in front of Secretariat, his favorite, (above) and with partner Jim Payne and their miniature horses (right).

Cawood with former governor John Y. Brown Jr...

...and with former governor
Martha Layne Collins.

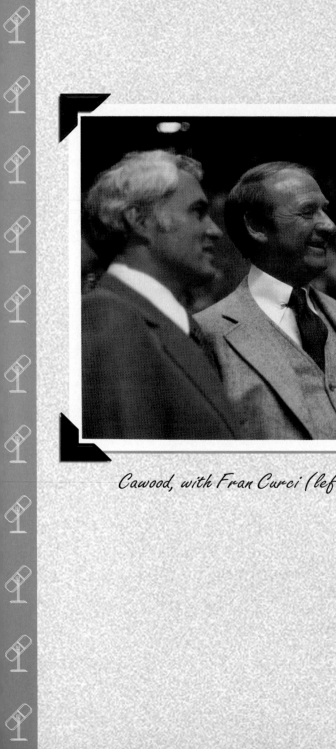

Cawood, with Fran Curci (left) and Joe B. Hall.

Cawood, Frances, Ralph Hacker and Sally Crutcher in Frankfort.

A laugh with former governor Wallace Wilkinson.

Bob Knight was one of many to honor Cawood.

CAWOOD
LIVING
LEGEND

Cawood and Rick Pitino drawing quite a crowd.

C.M. Newton thanked Cawood at his final football game.

Goodbye to the Commonwealth Stadium faithful.

The broadcast gang taking a break before the start of a game at Commonwealth.

The Voice of the Wildcats in the booth.

Audiences for
Pitino's postgame
radio show were
as big as many
Kentucky towns.

With a special bunch of Wildcats — (Clockwise) Deron Feldhaus, John Pelphrey, Sean Woods and Richie Farmer.

Young coaches Pitino and Curry flank a living legend in Kentucky athletics.

Cawood's final home game was an emotional evening.

*C.M. Newton honored Cawood and Frances
at the close of the '92 basketball season.*

*There's always time to sign
an autograph for a new fan.*

*"My Old Kentucky Home" was a fitting tribute to the
man who has meant so much to Kentucky athletics.*

Chapter 12

---

*The Stormy Years
Of Eddie Sutton*

The night Joe B. Hall announced his resignation, a bunch of us were in Dr. Singletary's room at a Denver hotel, throwing around who might be the next coach. Somebody suggested Dana Kirk, who that year was on the way to taking Memphis State to the Final Four in Rupp Arena. Dr. Singletary snorted and said, "I'm not going to hire any 50-year-old coach with a perm."

When the Final Four arrived in Lexington, the No. 1 topic in the hotel where the coaches were having their convention wasn't who was going to win the national championship, but who UK was going to hire. The search was really going awfully fast, it seemed to me. For some reason, the search committee and Cliff Hagan, then the UK athletics director, seemed to want to get it done right away. Another troubling thing about it was that some of the coaches who were interviewed said the process was vicious, insulting as hell.

At any rate, after interviewing Lute Olson, Gene Bartow, Lee Rose, Dickie Parsons and maybe a couple more, the university hired Eddie Sutton. When I reminded Dr. Singletary of his remarks in Denver about Dana Kirk, he laughed and said, "Well, Eddie has a perm, but he's only

49."

At the time, I didn't know Eddie very well. I had met him when his Arkansas team played UK in the 1978 Final Four in St. Louis, and I remember watching another one of his Razorback teams almost beat Louisville in the 1983 Mideast Regional in Knoxville. I also remember talking with him during an NCAA Tournament in Salt Lake City, neither one of us ever dreaming that he would someday be the UK coach. But I did know that he was a terrific coach. He took an Arkansas program that had never been worth a hoot and turned it into one of the nation's best. He was a winner, and I thought UK had made a heckuva choice.

When he was introduced to the press the Wednesday after the Final Four, he brought along Henry Iba, for whom he had played at Oklahoma State in the late 1950s. I thought that was a nice touch. Besides being a coaching legend who had won back-to-back NCAA titles in 1945 and '46, Mr. Iba had been one of Coach Rupp's closest friends. There were only a handful of coaches that Coach Rupp liked, and Mr. Iba certainly was one of them. They both belonged to a little cadre of coaches who were very powerful in the NCAA Tournament in the '40s, '50s and '60s.

Eddie sort of walked into a buzz-saw because the *Herald-Leader* broke its series about alleged wrongdoing in Hall's program just after practice began on October 15. That brought in the NCAA investigators, which created a huge distraction. Although the *Herald-Leader* was to win a

Pulitzer Prize for its series, the NCAA couldn't document some of the charges made in the series, such as $50 hand-shakes between boosters and players after games. Eventually the program got off with only a slight admonition for lack of co-operation, or something like that. A lot of coaches and writers laughed at the NCAA for not being able to find anything, and I think that explains why the NCAA took the hard line it did down the road. But we'll get to that in a moment.

Hall left Sutton with some pretty good players, but nobody expected the 1985-86 team to be as good as it was. It started three guards — Roger Harden, James Blackmon and Ed Davender — and didn't have a true center. Both the inside players, Kenny Walker and Winston Bennett, were natural forwards. But Sutton's patient offense and aggressive defense turned out to be perfect for that team. Everybody accepted his role and played it so well that the team wound up with a 32-4 record, UK's best won-lost mark since the championship year of 1978.

That team won both the SEC regular-season and tournament championships, and probably would have gone to the Final Four in Dallas had the NCAA Tournament committee not put two other SEC teams, Alabama and LSU, into Kentucky's region, the Southeast. I remember having dinner with a couple of members of the committee out in Kansas City after the pairings were announced. I kidded them about putting three SEC teams into the same region, but they explained they didn't see either LSU or Alabama going very far. Yet when Kentucky reached the regional semifinals in Atlanta, doggone it if the Cats weren't faced with the task of having to beat both Alabama and LSU a fourth time to reach the Final Four.

They handled 'Bama, 68-63, but fell short against LSU, 59-57. I don't care who you are, it's tough to beat a team four times in one season. I think that kind of embarrassed the tournament committee, and they changed the rule to say that no more than two teams from the same conference could be in the same region.

I'll always remember 1985-86 for the way Kenny Walker played. He was just magnificent. At 6'8", he should have been a small forward, but they asked him to play center and he played it well, even though I think his lack of experience at small forward hurt him when he got into the NBA. After getting poked in the eye again early in the season, he began wearing protective goggles, which became sort of his trademark. He was very graceful and he could really jump. I remember once, at Auburn, he joined in the dunking contests the players always like to have after practice. He usually didn't participate, but this time he did. And he put on an awesome show that had everybody laughing and shaking their heads. Later, of course, he won the dunking contest they have before the NBA All-Star game. They didn't call him "Sky" Walker for nothing.

That team probably should have gone to the Final Four

and maybe even farther. After all, it had beaten Louisville, which won the national title, by five points in December. But even though it fell a game short, Eddie won the award that The Associated Press gives each year to the man voted national Coach of the Year. I remember Happy Chandler, who always got close to the UK coaches, sent Eddie a one-word note: "Unpack."

Even then, however, everything wasn't perfect. Stories that Eddie had a drinking problem, which he admitted after he left UK, were beginning to surface.

I thought it was a little odd in view of the terrific season Eddie's first year had been that the university made no mention of a contract extension. Nor was UK throwing roses at Sutton. After the season he had — winning the SEC regular-season and tournament championships, making it to the NCAA's final eight and being named national Coach of the Year — I just couldn't figure it out. My personal feeling is that in view of Eddie's rumored drinking problems, the people at UK were going to take a wait-and-see attitude.

With Bennett, Davender and Blackmon returning, the prospects looked solid for 1986-87. However, Bennett suffered a serious knee injury in the preseason that knocked him out for the year. His loss was a terrible blow and somewhat, but only somewhat, tempered the excitement created by the arrival of Rex Chapman from Owensboro Apollo High. His father, Wayne, had played freshman ball at UK in 1963-64 before transferring to Western Kentucky, where he was a starter on those great Hilltopper teams led by Clem Haskins. But as good as Wayne was, Rex was much better. At 6'5", he was an exciting player who could take it to the hoop for spectacular dunks or pull up and drill the jumper.

The arrival of Rex at UK coincided with the arrival of the three-point shot in college basketball, a fortunate bit of timing for the Wildcats.

From day one, Rex was a phenom. He was called "Rex, the Boy King," and John McGill, then a sports columnist for *The Herald-Leader*, suggested the name of the city should be changed to "Rexington."

The rest of the nation discovered what all the fuss was about when the Wildcats played Louisville in Freedom Hall on national TV. Rex was fabulous that day, especially from three-point land, and he poured in 26 in an 85-51 UK win, still the worst loss ever suffered by a U of L team coached by Denny Crum. *Sports Illustrated* was so impressed that it ordered a story on Rex for the next week's issue.

However, Rex was up and down, as even great freshmen tend to be, and that team finished with a decent, but not spectacular, 18-11 record. The Cats then lost, 91-77, to a good Ohio State team, led by Dennis Hopson, in the first round of the Mideast Regional. Had Bennett been able to play, that team would have been much better and probably gone much further. But the good news was that Winston would be back for the 1987-88 season, joining Chapman, Davender, Rob Lock, Richard Madison, Cedric Jenkins and newcomer Eric Manuel on what promised to be a definite national championship contender. Sutton knew the team had that kind of potential, and he could barely restrain his enthusiasm going into the season.

The Cats got off to a 10-0 start and were ranked as high as No. 1 in some of the polls before hitting a snag in which they lost three of six games in the conference. About then is when stories began to surface that Sutton, the coach, and Chapman, his star player, weren't getting along. Sutton publicly criticized Chapman for his shot selection, and he was probably right. But Rex took it the wrong way, accusing Sutton of making public an internal problem that should have been kept private. I think their relationship might have affected the way the team played the rest of the season.

Even so, Kentucky won both the SEC regular-season and tournament titles and went into the NCAA with a 23-4 record and hopes for a trip to the Final Four in Seattle. Late in the season, the play of Manuel, a 6'6" swingman from Georgia who worked his way into the starting lineup, seemed to give the team a huge boost.

After beating both Southern and Maryland to play their way into the Southeast Regional in Birmingham, the Cats were upset by Villanova, 80-74. This wasn't one of Rollie Massimino's better teams, but the Wildcats from Philadelphia just outhustled the Wildcats from Lexington. Although Chapman led UK in scoring with a 19-point average and became the first UK player to ever pass 1,000 career points as a sophomore, he didn't seem happy. In fact, when Ralph Hacker asked Rex after the Villanova game if he might be thinking about entering the pro draft, he certainly didn't deny it.

Only a few weeks later, in April, an Emery Air Freight envelope spilled open on a conveyor belt in Los Angeles. Inside was $1,000. The envelope was addressed from Dwane Casey, one of Sutton's assistants, to Claud Mills, father of top recruit Chris Mills.

I first heard about it at the Daniel Boone Clinic in Harlan, where I had taken my father for some treatment. A guy came up to me and said, "What's going on at UK?"

I thought he was talking about the racial remarks Happy Chandler had made during a Board of Trustees meeting. But he told me about the envelope and then went outside to buy a *Herald-Leader* out of a rack so I could read the story. And so began what was to become one of the darkest chapters in UK basketball history and the only year of my 39 broadcasting Wildcat games that I really didn't enjoy. In fact, I was so miserable that, for the first time, I thought of quitting. But more about that in a moment.

Soon after the Emery story broke, the NCAA was back in Lexington for another investigation and this time I think they were determined to see to it that UK didn't get off the hook. Naturally, both the state's major papers, the *Herald-Leader* and *The Courier-Journal*, also began their own investigations. I'll always believe this is the final thing that pushed Chapman toward leaving school and entering the pro draft. I couldn't blame Rex, under the circumstances, but I also was sorry to see him go. He was a joy to watch because he had a lot of show-biz to him. He could really jump and, although he was not a great shooter, he was a great scorer.

The university president then was David Roselle, and the first thing he did was hire an investigator and give him complete access to everything UK had. I can't recall any university president anywhere ever having done that. When Chuck Smrt, the NCAA investigator, came in, everything went from bad to worse. Everybody in the basketball office was trying to cover their fanny, so everybody got a lawyer. Even some of the secretaries had lawyers. Along the way Eric Manuel was suspended because of allegations that he had cheated on his entrance exams.

It was just a miserable time. Every couple of days, it seemed that a new story or a new rumor or a new allegation would hit the papers. Then, while the team was playing Duke in the Tipoff Classic in its opening game, Dick Vitale said on national television that Sutton should resign for the good of the program. It was all downhill from there.

I was enraged that Vitale had the audacity to call for Eddie's resignation right at the outset of a season when none of the allegations surrounding the UK program had been proven. I had always liked Vitale, but I thought he had shown a total disregard for fairness and I felt I had to say that. I went on with a TV comment that began, "Dick Vitale is a jerk," and lambasted the TV commentator.

He later told me he was hurt by what I had to say and I told him he had hurt people with his outrageous comments. He was standing right in front my broadcast position during our conversation, and when neither of us was going to give in I just finally said, "Dick, please move on down press row, I'm afraid somebody in here might have bad aim."

I wasn't serious and was a little surprised when a body guard was furnished for Vitale at a UK game. I'm pleased that Dick and I have since patched up our differences and are friends again.

That 1988-89 team was Sutton's fourth at UK, and it was a fairly gifted club, even without Chapman and Manuel. It had an outstanding freshman swingman in Mills. LeRon Ellis, a 6'11" sophomore, brought size and agility in the middle. Eddie's son, Sean, was a better point guard than a lot of people realized, but Eddie got criticized for playing him ahead of freshman Richie Farmer, who became such a god as a high school player at Clay County that Eddie was forced to take him, even though he didn't think he could play Division I ball. Sophomore Reggie Hanson was a capable scorer and rebounder, and junior Derrick Miller could really bust it from outside. John Pelphrey and Deron Feldhaus were redshirt freshmen. Not a great team, but there have been many years when UK had worse talent.

As it turned out, the happiest moment of the season was when it was finally over. The team got off to a 2-5 start, fought back for an 11-10 record, then lost six consecutive SEC games. That sorry stretch eliminated any chances of a winning record. A 77-63 loss to Vanderbilt in the first round of the SEC Tournament made the final record 13-19, UK's first losing season since 1926-27. As fate would have it, the man who beat Sutton in what was to be his final game as UK coach was C.M. Newton, who had announced earlier in the year that he would accept Dr. Roselle's offer to succeed Hagan as UK's athletics director as soon as the season was over.

That was the only year Sutton did a poor coaching job at Kentucky, and I think the obvious reason was that he was distracted by controversy and his desire to keep his job. A lot of careers were on the line and everybody was trying to hang on. I wasn't sure of the outcome until I did a TV commentary after the season, saying what a good coach Eddie was. That night I got a call from somebody high up in the administration who told me, "He's gone, don't get involved, we're trying to get him to resign."

This guy also told me that it wasn't just because of the NCAA investigation, either. It wasn't long afterward — March 19, 1989, to be exact — that Eddie went out to Lexington CBS affiliate Channel 27 and made the live announcement that he was leaving.

I don't think we'll ever know exactly what happened, but I do have a few opinions. I believe there was $1,000 in that Emery envelope, but I don't believe Dwane Casey put it there. He's too smart, mainly, and he had just gotten back from a trip to the West Coast. It just doesn't make sense that he would do that, but somebody did, and I've heard two names mentioned as possibilities.

I also believe there was cheating on Eric Manuel's entrance exam, but I don't think he knew anything about it. Of all the tragic figures to come out of the whole mess, Eric was the most tragic. Had he admitted it, whether he did it or not, he would have gotten off lighter than he did. But he stuck to his guns and the NCAA ruled that he couldn't compete for any of their member institutions, forcing him to eventually end up at Oklahoma City, an NAIA school.

One more thing. I think David Roselle was a well-meaning, good man, but I also think he was the most naive college president ever involved in an NCAA investigation. He brought in that outside investigator and ordered him to conduct an investigation that was far, far more thorough than anything the NCAA had ever done or could do. He gave him access to everything. I think Roselle was hoping that by doing it that way, the NCAA would be lenient. Instead, the penalties that were finally handed down — two years' ineligibility for the NCAA Tournament and no live TV for a year were the crux of it — were about as severe as they could be. I had a lawyer, a guy who had studied all the evidence, tell me that if UK had fought the NCAA, the program would have only gotten a slap on the wrist. But in fairness, I'll also say this for Roselle: He purged the program. Today it's one of the cleanest in the country and I don't think it might have been before that.

After the penalties were handed down in May, all the players except Manuel were allowed to transfer and be eligible immediately at their new school. So Mills went to Arizona and Ellis to Syracuse. Sean Sutton left UK and transferred to Purdue for a brief stay, before returning to Lexington Community College for the rest of the year. He rejoined his father the following year at Oklahoma State. Miller and Hanson considered transferring, but finally decided to stay. So did Pelphrey, Feldhaus, Farmer and Sean Woods, who had been a Prop 48 case that season.

I stayed, too, but only after thinking seriously about hanging it up. Frances and I talked about it at great length. The program seemed to be totally in ashes and I had just gone through the most miserable year I'd ever spent behind a microphone. But I finally decided to come back for one more year. I thought it would be a coward's way out if I ran out on what promised to be the worst Kentucky team that anybody could remember.

Chapter 13

Happy Days Are Here Again

I thought it was really good news when we learned that C.M. Newton had been named to replace Cliff Hagan as the athletics director. I liked Cliff and I thought he did a good job in most areas. But if a change had to be made — and a lot of people thought it did — you couldn't have asked for a better guy than C.M., who had been a member of Coach Rupp's 1951 national championship team. Coach Rupp always liked C.M. He recommended him for the Transylvania job in the early 1950s, and he recommended him again for the Alabama job in 1968.

I had known C.M. at Transy and I got to know him even better when he was at Alabama. He got the 'Bama job mainly through Frank Rose, who had left Transy to become president at Alabama. Before C.M. took the job, he asked Bear Bryant, then Alabama's AD as well as its football coach, if there would be any recruiting restrictions. Meaning, of course, could he recruit blacks? The Bear told him he could recruit anybody he wanted, so long as he was a good person and a good student. That opened the doors for C.M. to build the program by recruiting the best black players from within the state. He got guys like Wendell Hudson, Leon Douglas, Charles Cleveland, T.R. Dunn and Reggie King. He had some great teams there, and they had been just a doormat before that. Later on, he also did a fine job at Vanderbilt, largely by taking a lot of Kentucky kids that UK didn't want.

But beyond C.M.'s record as a coach — and I think, by the way, that he someday deserves to be inducted into the Hall of Fame — I've always been amazed by his reputation for being one of the most honest and decent men in college athletics. I got to know some of the nation's most influential movers and shakers through my work with the NCAA Tournament Radio Network, and I never heard anybody say anything bad about him. He's just so well-respected that I knew he was going to be the perfect guy for Kentucky.

One of the first things C.M. did after officially coming to work on April 1 was to meet with the basketball team. He promised the players he would find them a good coach and he urged them to stay instead of transferring. He also made it a point to travel all over the state and urge the fans to hang in there. I give him a lot of credit for holding the fan support together at a time when just about everybody, myself included, was disillusioned and depressed. He was straight with everybody, which is the only way C.M. knows how to do it. He said the penalties would be harsh, but he promised that UK would put the pieces back together and be stronger than ever.

As far as the new basketball coach was concerned, C.M. told me he had four criteria: The guy had to want the job, he had to be a proven winner, he had to have a "Mr. Clean" reputation and he had to favor the up-tempo style that Kentucky fans had come to love years earlier under Coach Rupp. I think his first choice was Pat Riley, but Pat told him on the phone that he didn't want to leave the Lakers at that time. Rick Pitino also was on C.M.'s short list, but he said he wouldn't even discuss it until after the New York Knicks had finished their season. C.M. didn't want to wait that long, so he brought in both Lute Olson of Arizona and P.J. Carlesimo of Seton Hall, but they both decided to stay put. By this time the Knicks' season was over and Pitino, who was having problems with general manager Al Bianchi, agreed to come have a look. They even had a press conference at Wildcat Lodge in which Rick said only that he would go back home and think about it.

"I don't believe he's going to take it," I told C.M. as we were walking together outside Wildcat Lodge after the press conference.

"We've got him," C.M. said.

And they did, too.

I didn't really know Rick, but I had called the game on the radio when his Providence team played Syracuse in the 1987 Final Four in New Orleans. My color man for that game was Dave Gavitt, the former Providence coach who then was the Big East Conference commissioner. Gavitt was a big Pitino fan and had told me all about Rick. "You've never seen a team shoot the three like they do," he told me, and he was right.

Even though I knew Providence had manhandled an outstanding Alabama team — maybe one of Wimp Sanderson's best — and beaten Georgetown to get to the Final Four, I was surprised both by their bombs-away style and, frankly, their lack of great talent. At the first break during the Syracuse game, I took off the headphones and told Dave Gavitt that Providence had only one player, Billy Donovan, who might — might — have been able to start for UK that year. I don't think I was exaggerating because UK's starters in '87 were Rex Chapman, Ed Davender, James Blackmon, Richard Madison and Cedric Jenkins. I know they had more talent than that Providence team.

Well, of course, Rick took the job. He said all the right things at his press conference. He promised to press, run and play exciting, entertaining basketball. He mentioned the *Sports Illustrated* cover story about Kentucky's problems — "Kentucky's Shame," was how *SI* titled it — and he promised that the next time UK was on the *SI* cover, it would be a picture of the Wildcats cutting down the nets after winning the national championship. After the press conference, he went to see this WVLK disc jockey, Robert Lindsay, who had vowed to sit on a billboard until UK hired a new coach. He found Lindsay, still on the billboard, and told him he could finally get down.

UK gave Rick a seven-year contract instead of the usual five because, as C.M. said, it wouldn't be fair to hold the first two seasons, when the team would be on probation, against him. I think everybody was expecting disaster. I picked UK to win eight games in 1989-90 and told Rick that if he won 10 he should be the national Coach of the Year. It was that bleak. The top four players were gone. LeRon Ellis had transferred to Syracuse. Chris Mills had gone to Arizona after the NCAA ruled him ineligible to play at Kentucky. Eric Manuel was in limbo because the NCAA had ruled that he couldn't play at any of their member schools (he eventually wound up at an NAIA school, Oklahoma City). Sean Sutton dropped out of school and almost went to Purdue, but changed his mind.

That left senior Derrick Miller and junior Reggie Hanson as the nucleus of a team that also had sophomores John Pelphrey, Deron Feldhaus, Richie Farmer and Sean Woods. Heck, they only had eight scholarship players, which forced Pitino to appeal to the student body for walkons. He got some, but even then Donovan, who had come along as one of his assistants, had to suit up and participate in some of the scrimmages.

I remember thinking back to Pitino's first press conference in Lexington and I recall how fragile looking I thought he was to be undertaking such a gigantic rebuilding program. I wouldn't have been so concerned about him being too frail if I had known then what I know now. Rick Pitino is about as frail as an Eastern Kentucky coal truck on a narrow mountain road.

It didn't take long to see the qualities that make Rick such an outstanding coach:

• He's a really combative fellow, and the team picked up that attitude. Before Rick came along, they had been losers and they thought of themselves as losers. Under him, though, they became warriors. When UK was playing Indiana that year in the Hoosier Dome, Rick saw Bobby Knight chewing on an official as they were leaving the floor at halftime so he grabbed another official and did his own chewing. At LSU, he almost got into a fistfight with Dale Brown. The players picked up on that.

• He's a master psychologist and motivator. He rode Pelphrey hard, for example, because he knew Pelphrey needed it and could take it. But Feldhaus, on the other hand, is more sensitive, so he handled him differently. Treating players equally doesn't necessarily mean treating them the same, and Rick is a master of that.

• It's amazing how well he prepares his teams. In our pre-game shows, I was amazed at how well he had analyzed the game and the opponent. I thought I knew a little something about basketball, but this guy has taught me a lot.

• His teams always are so well-conditioned. His first season, the players were shocked by his conditioning program. It was easily the roughest any of them had ever experienced. He brought in Rock Oliver from Pittsburgh as his strength coach and Rock turned out to be a real drill sergeant. The players all were sick, but they also got a lot of weight off. You can't play in Pitino's system if you're not in the best shape of your life.

• Finally, he's a very intelligent guy. I think he probably understood the three-point shot, and what it could do for a team, quicker than anybody in the game. His first Kentucky team was exactly like that Providence team he took to the Final Four. The only bad shot for them was when they couldn't see the rim. They'd fire it from anywhere at the drop of a hat. Billy Reed christened them "Pitino's Bambinos" before the season because they were so young, but John McGill, then with the *Herald-Leader*, changed that to "Pitino's Bombinos." It was apt, too, because that first team really bombed away.

About three weeks before the opening game of that first season, Rick called and asked if I would mind doing the post-game show from courtside instead of the locker room. He thought that would be a good way for the coaches' wives and the players' friends and families to kill time while they were waiting. I said that was fine with me. Coach Rupp used to do his post-game show from courtside until so many fans began to crowd around that it got uncomfortable, so we moved it under the stands in the old Coliseum. But Pitino, ever the showman, had a new twist. He wanted to broadcast it over the P.A. system. At first we had a few hundred stick around, but then it grew into the thousands. The crowds got so big that Chris Cameron, the UK sports information director, took a survey and figured out that the population of the

Pitino post-game show was equal to the 16th biggest attendance in all of college basketball that season. The big post-game crowds really seemed to enjoy Rick, and I think the showman in him came out before a live audience. It also helped that Kentucky seldom lost in Rupp Arena. It was true then and it is still true.

I really enjoyed that first season. Talk about a roller-coaster. I went from the season I hated the most to one that I loved as much as any. In fact, at the time, I ranked that first Pitino team right below Rupp's Runts on my list of the teams I enjoyed the most. They were just so darned much fun and they worked so hard to overcome their deficiencies. The next time you hear anybody talking about character, bring up that team because those guys were loaded with it.

The first clue that they might do better than anybody expected came in the Big Four Classic in the Hoosier Dome, when they took a heavily favored Indiana team right down to the wire before losing, 71-69. But then, after going 3-1, they went out to Kansas and absolutely got crushed, 150-95.

I think right about then everybody was thinking, uh-oh, this might turn out to be the nightmare we were expecting. And when they lost five in a row in late December and early January, another losing season seemed unavoidable. But those guys hung in there and took a 14-12 record into their final two games. They lost both, to Ole Miss and Notre Dame on the road, but that didn't really matter. They already had won a special place in my heart and, I think, the hearts of UK fans everywhere.

I guess my favorite moment of that season came against LSU in Rupp Arena on February 15. That LSU team probably had as much raw talent as any team the league had seen in years — two seven-footers in Stanley Roberts and Shaquille O'Neal, not to mention an All-American guard in Chris Jackson. Earlier, they had beaten the Cats, 94-81, in Baton Rouge. This time, however, Kentucky turned the tables, withstanding a sensational late shooting exhibition by Jackson for a 100-95 win. But the incredible thing was, Kentucky had them down by 23 in the first half!

The crowd was great that night. In fact, it was great all year. That rag-tag team got the fans excited in a way they hadn't been since the team moved to Rupp Arena. That team won only one conference game on the road, against Florida, but it was unbeaten in the league at home, which I thought was quite an accomplishment.

While being off TV for that one season may have hurt Rick's recruiting, it was another lucky break for me. With no television, UK fans who weren't lucky enough to have tickets in Rupp Arena had to listen to my radio broadcasts. So many Kentucky fans turned down the sound when the games were on TV and listened to radio, I think I had accidentally fallen into the habit of calling the game as if the listeners could watch it along with me. I went back several years and listened to some old tapes and discovered that my style had changed. I went right back to a pure radio call and I've been doing it ever since.

In the middle of that basketball season, C.M. pulled off another stunning hiring coup. The first choice to replace Jerry Claiborne as football coach had been Mike Shanahan, an assistant with the Denver Broncos, but he decided at the last minute to stay in the pros. After Shanahan pulled out, nobody knew what UK would do next. There was some support for Mike Gottfried, who had resigned under pressure at Pittsburgh, but there also were some questions about the circumstances under which he left.

At the Sugar Bowl in New Orleans, C.M. contacted Bill Curry and visited him in Curry's hotel room. Although Curry had taken the Crimson Tide to the Sugar Bowl in only his third season, earning him conference Coach of the Year honors, he was unhappy in Tuscaloosa. Some of the old guard down there just wouldn't accept him because he played at Georgia Tech, which had been a hated 'Bama rival, and because he didn't have any connection to Coach Bryant. Hadn't played for him or coached under him, that sort of thing. That sounds sort of crazy, I know, but there was enough of this feeling around to make Curry feel uncomfortable. No matter what he did, it wasn't enough for the 'Bama faithful.

So Curry told C.M. that he might be interested, but that he didn't really want to think about it until after Alabama's Sugar Bowl game against Miami. The Tide lost to the Hurricanes, who were declared the national champions after

Notre Dame's win over top-ranked Colorado in the Orange Bowl. After Curry returned to Tuscaloosa, he met with Newton. The timing was perfect for both sides. Curry wanted out and UK needed another Mr. Clean coach to replace Claiborne. On January 8, 1990, UK held a press conference to introduce Curry as its new coach.

To tell you the truth, I was shocked. I didn't think I'd live long enough to see the day when Kentucky could hire the Alabama football coach. Soon after the hiring, Curry met with the press in the Wildcat Den at Commonwealth Stadium. When he met me, he told me pretty much the same thing that Pitino had when he was hired — that he felt he knew me because he had listened to some of my calls while on the road during recruiting trips. He's a charmer, Curry is, and I liked what he said at that press conference: He didn't believe in excuses, he wanted his team to perform at the championship level, and academics were a top priority. Then Curry went out and got what I thought was a great recruiting class, under the circumstances.

It would have been nice if Curry could have enjoyed the same kind of debut season that Pitino did, but I think it's just harder in football because of the numbers involved. His first team finished 4-7, which wasn't bad, all things considered. I figured they would have to do well in the non-conference part of the schedule to have any chance at a decent record, but they surprised me. After winning only one of their non-conference games, the opener against Central Michigan,

Curry's first team won three SEC games, including a big win over Georgia in Commonwealth Stadium. Although the record wasn't quite as good as expected, I think the fans liked Curry's style, which was more wide-open than it had been under the conservative Claiborne, and they really liked the recruits, most of whom were red-shirted.

At any rate, I can't think of any school in the country that had two more attractive coaches than UK, and the lion's share of the credit belonged to C.M. Newton. I did a TV commentary in which I said that if I saw Newton in Vegas, I'd follow him to the gambling tables and stack my chips right next to his. He was on a roll in the hiring department, no doubt about it.

After putting Curry's first season to bed, I turned my attention to Pitino's second season. Once again the team wouldn't be eligible for post-season play, because of the NCAA sanctions, but at least they were back on TV, which was a lot more important than a lot of people may realize. To those of us who have been around for a while, tradition means the Rupp era, the Hall era, all that. But to young recruits, tradition only means, "How many times were you on TV last year?" During that first season, Rick mentioned to me several times how tough it was to recruit when you weren't on TV. He was lucky to get a player as good as Jamal Mashburn, his first big-time, blue-chip recruit. With Mashburn, though, he was able to overcome the TV thing by playing on his background as a native New Yorker and the former coach of the Knicks.

Although Rick had made a believer out of me, I was still cautious when I predicted the record for 1990-91. I said they'd win 17. Once again, though, I was one of many who underestimated the team's character and its desire to achieve. With Mashburn replacing Derrick Miller in the starting lineup, the Cats rolled to a 22-6 record that earned them the No. 9 ranking in the final Associated Press poll. The old Kentucky homeboys — Pelphrey, Feldhaus, Hanson and Farmer — all had outstanding years, as did Woods and Jeff Brassow.

A couple of games stick out as pivotal. When they beat a good Cincinnati team, 75-71, on November 28 in UC's Shoemaker Center, it proved to the players that they could win on the road. Another road win, 81-80 over Georgia in Athens on January 2, set the right tone for the conference season. The final league record, 14-4, was the best in the SEC, but the conference didn't recognize them as regular-season champions because of the NCAA probation. In fact, the league listed UK at the bottom of the standings, with an asterisk, which struck some fans as unfair, considering that in football they had put Florida at the top of the standings, with an asterisk, even though the Gators also were on proba-tion. After the final home game, a 114-93 win over Auburn, C.M. declared 'em to be No. 1 in the SEC and announced a parade through Lexington in their honor. They deserved at least that much. All five starters had averaged in double figures and Pelphrey was named to the all-conference team.

I just have to put in a word here about Pelphrey, Farmer, and Feldhaus. Coming out of high school, none of them was avidly recruited by Sutton's staff, even though they all were all-staters. Feldhaus, who played for his dad, Allen, at Mason County, was recruited at the 11th hour. Pelphrey, from Paintsville, was on his way to Vanderbilt — C.M. had really wanted him — but he jumped when UK offered him a scholarship because, like most kids in Kentucky, he had always dreamed of playing for the Cats. And as for Farmer, Sutton's staff thought he was too small and too slow. They questioned his defense and whether he could play offense without the ball. They finally took him only because there was such a public uproar, especially in Eastern Kentucky, where Richie was a high school legend.

But you know what? Those kids all wanted to play for UK so badly that they over-achieved. They were lucky that Pitino came along when he did, and Rick was lucky to have them. Years from now, I'm confident those three will be remembered as warmly as all the All-Americans.

It was during that season that I received what I consider to be the highest honor of my life — having my own banner hung in Rupp Arena. It's the only banner hanging there that isn't for a UK player or coach. And believe me, I was completely surprised when I found out about it. I had no inkling it was in the works. I also have no doubts about who was behind it — Rick Pitino. I can't thank him enough. I've been fortunate to receive a lot of honors, but like I said, this is the one that means the most to me.

Chapter 14

"And Now They Come to Me..."

I've been connected with UK for so long that a lot of people are surprised to learn that my favorite sporting event isn't the Final Four. Don't get me wrong, I love the Final Four because, as I mentioned earlier, I've sort of watched it grow from a modest event into a real classic. But if you told me I could only cover one thing in any given year, it would be the Kentucky Derby.

I liked horses even before I knew anything about basketball. My mother really liked horses and I remember her reading me stories about them when I was little. My grandad always had good pleasure horses. He gave me a pony when I was four years old, and I had either a pony or a horse from then until I went away to college. I took my first formal riding lessons at Centre, and I finally found something in sports that I could do pretty well. We'd have these horse shows out on a farm and I won every class for three years. Also, in the summers, I'd show other people's horses at some of the county fairs around the state.

A couple of my buddies at Centre, Frank Gernert and Ben Lemaster, were both from Louisville and they liked to go to Churchill Downs whenever they could. They taught me to read a Daily Racing Form, then took me to the races for the first time at Keeneland. That was in the spring of 1947 and a terrible thing happened to me: I won some money. The next year, Frank took me to Louisville to see my first Derby. The winner was the great Citation, who went on to win the Triple Crown. A lot of old-timers still think he was the best Derby winner ever.

I didn't call my first race until the spring of 1954. An industrious salesman at WLEX managed to sell not just the race of the day from Keeneland, but a tape-delay of the whole darned card. In those days they only had a 10-day meet, with eight races a day, so here I was, a guy who had never called a race in his life, suddenly having to do 80 of them over 10 days. Talk about nervous: I couldn't eat, I couldn't sleep. It's tough to break in at the top, but that's what you do when you call races at Keeneland.

I finally went to J.B. Faulconer, my UK announcing colleague. He had done a lot of racing — in fact, he retired as an announcer so he could become Keeneland's publicity director, which in turn led him to become a prominent breeder and racing official. He told me to forget about the numbers on the saddle clothes, because you couldn't see them when the horses were on the backstretch, and concentrate on memorizing the silks that the jockeys wore.

Well, I didn't know if I could memorize the silks of 10 or 12 horses in the 10 minutes from the time the horses came on the track until they were loaded in the starting gate, so at first I started trying to do it by the numbers. But J.B.

was right; you couldn't see the darned things. So I began going to the jockeys' room before every race so I could get a head start on memorizing the silks. That just about killed me because Keeneland didn't have an elevator in those days so it was up and down the stairs between every race. I didn't know it at the time, but doing those 80 races that spring was the best thing that ever happened to me as far as learning to call the races was concerned.

I'd have to say that calling a horse race is about the hardest job in sports announcing. It's a lot different from basketball or football. The action is so far away from you, for one thing. There's also more chances to make mistakes because it's easy to get the colors mixed up. Everybody who has ever called a race — and I'm even talking about such greats as Bryan Field and Clem McCarthy — dreads calling the wrong leader or the wrong winner. Believe it or not, though, the classic races are easier to do than, say, your average six-furlong claiming event. For one thing, the longer races — the Derby, for example, is a mile and a quarter — give you more time to sort things out. For another, the horses in stakes races are generally better known and run truer to form.

Over the years, I've seen race calling change a lot. The guys I grew up with — Field and McCarthy and some others — did it with a certain flair and style. I suppose I tried to do it that way, too. When the horses would turn for home, I'd say, "And now they come to me." I'm not sure when I started that, but it kind of became my trademark. Today it seems that a lot of the race callers are more like track announcers — very accurate, but very clinical. In racing, though, accuracy is what counts the most, especially to all those people in the stands clutching their parimutuel tickets.

After going to WHAS, I worked my first Kentucky Derby in the spring of 1957. My job Derby week was to set up in this little grassy area on the backstretch, near the chute where the horses went on the track to work out. Our equipment wasn't very sophisticated back then, so the only way I would know to go on the air was to listen to the radio. When I'd heard them say, "And now let's go to Cawood Ledford on the backstretch...," I'd begin talking and keep going for as long as I was supposed to go. But otherwise, I had no other way to contact the station, which created a little problem for me on Derby Day.

The night before the race, I gave $10 to Dave Martin, one of my cohorts, and told him to bet it on the Calumet Farm entry of Gen. Duke and Iron Leige. I loved Gen. Duke, who was the favorite that year. But when I got to the track the next day, I heard that Gen. Duke had been scratched because of an injury. Since I had no way to get in touch with Dave, I kissed my $10 good-bye. But wouldn't you know it? Iron Leige, the other half of the entry, won the race after Bill Shoemaker, who was riding Gallant Man, misjudged the finish line and raised up in the irons, giving Iron Leige the break he needed to win. I won my bet, but only because of pure, blind luck.

The 1961 Derby was the first one I called for WHAS, and I did it from then until the early 1980s, when I finally stopped because I just wasn't doing enough races to stay sharp. For a few years in the 1970s, I called it for the CBS Radio Network. I've enjoyed every single Derby I've ever covered, but I suppose the first one always is the one you remember the most.

The winner that year was Carry Back, which was fitting because he's so typical of the kind of stories that make the Derby so special. His owner, Jack Price, had paid only $400 for his mother, the mare Joppy, and it cost him only another $300 to breed her to a cheap stallion named Saggy. Out of that modest breeding came Carry Back, whose come-from-behind style won him a lot of fans that spring. He came to Churchill Downs off wins in the Florida Derby and Flamingo, the two biggest Derby prep races in Florida, and immediately Price made a lot of people mad, including yours truly, by saying that to him, the Kentucky Derby was "just another $100,000 race." Everybody hated him for that, wanted to tar-and-feather him, but that just caused Price to needle much harder.

Well, Carry Back won, coming from so far off the pace that, early in the race, even Price, who also was his trainer, thought he was hopelessly beaten. Jack told me later that he had told jockey Johnny Sellers to stay six or eight lengths behind the leaders. Well, as the race unfolded, there were two clumps of horses running in front of Carry Back, but Sellers wasn't aware of the first group, so he stayed six or eight lengths behind the second group. You can imagine his surprise when he got up next to the second group only to see another group still ahead. But Carry Back made it, running down Crozier in the stretch.

The best part of that story, however, was what happened in the following years. Jack Price, who had mocked the Derby, became its biggest fan. He said that everywhere he took Carry Back after that, the only race that people ever asked him about was the Kentucky Derby. He became such a believer that long after Carry Back had died, he allowed the Derby winner's remains to be brought back to Louisville and buried outside the Derby museum. I don't think Jack ever missed a Derby after he won it.

That's the great thing about the Derby. They've been running the thing for well over a century — the 1992 running was the 118th — and every one seems to have its own charming story. My favorite part of the Derby is being out on the backstretch in the mornings the week before the race. It's a great time of year, especially when the weather is nice and everything is turning green or blooming, and the optimism is so fresh and real in every barn that you can just feel it. Every year there are different stories and new characters, but also people that you've gotten to know as old friends, even if you only see them once a year. I love a cup of coffee any time, but it always tastes a little better on a crisp morning the week before the Derby.

Besides the horsemen, I also enjoy the writers who come in to cover the Derby. Col. Matt Winn, who ran Churchill Downs from the early 1900s until his death in 1949, turned the race into a national event largely because of the way he courted the press, especially the big-name writers from New York City. Guys like Damon Runyon and Grantland Rice wrote great, colorful stuff about the Derby in the 1920s, '30s, and '40s. They were before my time, of course, but I did get to know Red Smith, who was the best sportswriter of my lifetime and a tremendous lover of racing. I remember one year when it was raining on the backstretch and about 30 of us were crowded into a little workroom that was built to handle maybe eight. We were talking about how the Derby is the only race of the year that a lot of guys will cover and Red said, "A Derby expert is just a baseball writer with a pair of borrowed binoculars." I loved that line.

Of all the Derbys I've covered, the best race was the duel between Northern Dancer and Hill Rise in 1964. They hooked each other all the way to the wire before the little horse, Northern Dancer, finally won. He went on, of course, to become the most successful breeding stallion the sport has ever known. So that was the best race, but the best performance has to be Secretariat in 1973. His time, 1:59 2/5, set a Derby record that still stands.

Secretariat already was a story when he got to

Louisville. Seth Hancock, who had taken over at Claiborne Farm the previous year after his father, Bull Hancock, died of cancer, put together a syndicate that agreed to pay Secretariat's owner, Mrs. Penny Tweedy, $6.08 million, then a record, in exchange for lifetime breeding rights to the colt after he was retired to stud. Seth was very young then, only in his early 20s, and this was his first big deal. He was subjected to a lot of second-guessing, especially after Secretariat finished third in the Wood Memorial, his final race before the Derby. During Derby week, there were all kinds of rumors floating around, including one started by Jimmy "The Greek" Snyder, that Secretariat was lame, or something like that. That was completely false, of course, but it added to the pressure on everybody in the Secretariat camp.

Well, if you go back and analyze that Derby, you'll see that it might be even more impressive than the 31-length victory in the Belmont Stakes that capped off Secretariat's Triple Crown. He ran every quarter mile faster than the one before. When you accelerate all the way in a race like the Derby, you've got to be something special. And he was. I became such a Secretariat fan that it was almost like hero-worship. After Seth and I became good friends, he gave me a couple of Secretariat's shoes and a bit of his mane preserved in plexiglass. I've got them in my office at home, and I prize them about as highly as anything I've collected over the years.

I've had such great fun with the Derby that it more than makes up for the fact that I never got to cover an Olympics. That's the one thing I would have liked to have covered, but never did. I didn't miss any of the others. I've covered the Indianapolis 500, the World Series, The Masters and U.S. Open golf tournaments.

If you asked me to pick one that stands out, I suppose it would be the first heavyweight championship fight I ever covered. That was on January 25, 1964, when Cassius Clay, the so-called "Louisville Lip," took on Sonny Liston, the glowering champion, in Miami Beach.

I had started interviewing Clay when he was an up-and-coming amateur in the late 1950s, and I got the first interview with him when he returned to Louisville after winning the light-heavyweight gold medal at the 1960 Olympics in Rome. So before that first fight with Liston, WHAS sent me down to Miami Beach to do a TV special. I arrived a week ahead of the fight and Bill Faversham, the managing partner of the group of Louisville businessmen who were backing Clay's pro career, was great to me. He took aside Angelo Dundee, Clay's trainer, and told him that Larry Boeck, who was covering the fight for *The Courier-Journal*, and I were to be treated like family. He gave us total access, and that really teed off a guy who was down there covering the fight for ABC Radio. Howard Cosell is who I'm talking about. That was the first time I'd met him, and he couldn't stand it that I could take my tape recorder and go anywhere.

Using a film crew from a Miami station, I finished the special, which we called "Float Like a Butterfly, Sting Like a Bee." That was what Clay and Bundini Brown, Clay's alter ego, liked to chant all the time. I left to do a couple of UK basketball games, but then I caught a plane back on the day of the fight. I had missed the weigh-in, and when I got to press headquarters, all the big-name boxing writers — Jimmy Cannon and all those guys — were guessing they were going to call the fight off because of the crazy way Clay had been acting at the weigh-in. He was rolling his eyes and screaming and his blood pressure was off the charts. Fear, the way everybody figured it. When I heard all that, I called Faversham. "That's just Cassius," he told me. "He's fine. He's sleeping in the next room right now."

Well, of course, that night Clay made boxing history when Liston failed to answer the bell for the seventh round. To tell you the truth, I wasn't surprised. I thought he would win. In fact, when Coach Rupp had said Clay didn't have a chance, I tried to get him to bet me $10. "Well," he said, "let's make it something worthwhile. How about a color TV?"

He was just trying to get me to back off, but when I called his bluff, he wouldn't bet. The next time I saw him, he was laughing like hell. "By gawd, Cawood," he said, "you were right about that boy."

The day after the fight, when I was doing a one-on-one interview with Cassius, he told me he had joined the Muslim faith and was changing his name to Muhammad Ali. The only thing that kept me from getting a "scoop" was that about 50 or 60 reporters were standing there, eavesdropping. By the time I got my film back to WHAS, the whole world knew about it. But we got an even bigger "scoop" a few years later when Ali told one of my WHAS colleagues, Charlie Mastin, that he was going to refuse induction into the draft because he "didn't have nothin' against them Viet Cong."

When he refused to step forward and be drafted, the boxing people stripped him of his title and refused to let him fight for almost four years at the peak of his career. That was a shame because, in his prime, Ali was the greatest athlete I ever saw, in addition to being the most interesting and charismatic person I've ever worked with. When he came back, he was never the same as he was before they took his title away.

Another guy I always enjoyed was Pete Rose. During his days with the Cincinnati Reds, both as a manager and a player, he was unfailingly nice to me. He would sit down sometimes and we'd go as long as an hour, talking about baseball. I think Pete enjoyed it, maybe because he and I had a mutual interest in horse racing. I admired him so much as a player because he never gave less than 100 percent. It was just refreshing to see a guy hustle and play his guts out, just like he was a rookie trying to make the team. I really felt bad about all the trouble he got into later over his gambling and his tax problems. That was regrettable, but I'll tell you this: It shouldn't keep him out of the Hall of Fame.

I should also mention a couple of basketball coaches. In the early days when I worked for WHAS, I also did some Louisville games. Even went on the road with them a few times. The Cardinals' coach then was Peck Hickman, who brought 'em out of the small time when he won the 1956 NIT, then as important a title as the NCAA. But the guy who took U of L to the top level was Denny Crum. After he won his second national title in 1986, he told me the first one, in 1980, was more important to him because every coach, in the recesses of his mind, worries that he'll get stuck with the tag of not being able to win the big one. But Denny not only moved U of L up, he kept the program near the top, which is even harder.

There's no question that Crum's a good coach, but he's also a good guy. He's a real straight-shooter. If you ask him something, he'll tell you what he thinks. Once he did me a great favor. We were talking about hunting and fishing and the outdoors when he mentioned an author named Louis L'Amour. I'd never heard of him, so a couple of weeks later Crum sent me one of his paperbacks. I read it and loved it and became such a fan, like Denny, that I guess I've read just about every one L'Amour ever wrote.

Another guy who's always been super to me is Bobby Knight. A lot of UK fans won't believe this, but he reminds me of Coach Rupp a lot. Like Adolph, Knight is so driven to win that he just doesn't know how to walk away from a loss. Also like Adolph, Knight's a character who's one of the most entertaining men in coaching. I've seen a side of Bobby that not many people get to see, and that's the side of him that just likes to sit down and talk and have a good time. He can be really funny, and he's just so doggoned smart.

I'll always remember the 1979 Final Four — that was the one that had Michigan State's Magic Johnson going against Indiana State's Larry Bird in the championship game — as the one where Bobby was my analyst on NBC Radio. He was as good a color man as I've ever worked with. We announcers have a little inside joke about working with coaches who show up carrying a briefcase that, when they open it up, has only a sandwich inside.

Well, Bobby was just the opposite of that. He had notes and he had interviewed other coaches. Really prepared himself, just as he does in coaching. I had so much fun that my only regret is that we couldn't have worked together more. He's just the kind of person who's going to be good at whatever he does. And, of course, he can flat-out coach basketball, whether all his detractors want to admit it or not.

Chapter 15

The Last Cup Of Coffee

When I finally decided that the 1991-92 season would be my last one, the first time I mentioned it to anyone other than Frances was on June 4, 1991, when Jim Host and I met for lunch at the Lexington Country Club to discuss some projects. "This will be it," I told him. I don't think Jim was really surprised because we had talked about it previously, even if only in a casual way. He had always told me he wanted me to do it as long as I was breathing, which I appreciated, but I just felt the time had come.

Jim and I agreed that certain people would have to be notified right away: Ralph Gabbard of Channel 27 and Ralph Hacker of WVLK, who were Jim's partners in owning the UK broadcast rights; C.M. Newton, Rick Pitino and Bill Curry at UK; and my staff and several of my close friends. Jim said he would set up the meetings.

By Wednesday, June 26, Jim had everyone lined up except Curry, who was in Hawaii on vacation. First we met with the two Ralphs, who I think were both surprised. Then we went out to UK and met with C.M., then with Rick. We had already talked with C.M. on the phone so that was more of a courtesy call. We met with Rick and told him of my decision and the first thing he said was, "I thought I had a few more years with you, but I guess we'll just have to go out and win the NCAA Championship this season." He damned near did it, too. We called Bill in Hawaii. The news got out when Channel 27 did a live cut-in on its noon news show and WVLK went on the air with it. That afternoon, after it had been on WVLK, some guys were going by on a fire truck. When they saw me, they slowed down and yelled, "Don't go!"

The next day, it was on the front page of both the *Herald-Leader* and *The Courier-Journal*, which sort of surprised me. I didn't think it was THAT big of a story. But what really surprised me was the mail that began coming in...and never really stopped. I thought there would be a reaction at first and maybe another one toward the end, but they just kept coming...wonderful, sentimental, touching letters from UK fans everywhere.

Back then, the end seemed so far away that I just decided to block it out of my mind and try to approach the last season just as I had the previous 38. I wanted it to be as good as any, from a professional standpoint, so I could really have the feeling that I had gone out at my peak.

At the start of Curry's second season, I predicted a 7-4 record in my newspaper, *Cawood on Kentucky*, but it didn't take me long to know that, as usual, I had been too optimistic. In the opener, the team struggled to a 23-20 win over Miami of Ohio, a team from the Mid-American Conference. The next week, the Cats went to Bloomington and outplayed

Indiana for 35 minutes, only to weaken at the end and let the Hoosiers escape with a 13-10 win. They looked like a team waiting to get beat, and that told me right there that Curry still hadn't been able to exorcise that deep-rooted losing attitude that has plagued UK football for so long.

They won only two games the rest of the way, against Kent State and Cincinnati, and went 0-7 in the SEC, even losing to Vanderbilt and Mississippi State, a couple of traditional doormats who were under first-year coaches Gerry DiNardo and Jackie Sherrill, respectively.

On the Monday before the final football game against Tennessee, we did Pitino's first "Big Blue Line" show from his restaurant, Bravo Pitino's, and he immediately jumped on the "One More Year" bandwagon. He told me that instead of stopping with 39 years, I should retire with a nice, round 40. He kept that up the whole season; it became kind of a running joke between us. I played along with it, but I knew there was no way. I had gone too far to turn back.

Then, on Curry's "Big Blue Line" show that Thursday, he became the first — and only — UK coach to ask me to address the team before a game. I must admit that I was pretty nervous on that Saturday, November 19, when, after I had taped Curry's pregame show at the Athens-Boonesborough Holiday Inn and the team had eaten its pregame meal, I stood before those 100 or so young men who had gone through such a tough year. First Curry got up and gave me a glowing introduction. Then the players gave me a standing ovation, which kind of got to me. When they finally settled down, I just decided to speak from the heart. My first line was that I had picked Tennessee to beat their ass that day, but I wished I could take it back after seeing the courageous way they had played the previous week in a 36-25 road loss to Florida, the SEC champion.

Then I told 'em about some of UK's great upsets of Tennessee. I talked about the great game Lou Michaels had played back in 1957 when the Cats, who had gone into the game as 23-point underdogs, upset the Vols at Stoll Field. And about how Fran Curci, knowing that the 1981 game against the Vols was to be his last, had told Johnny Majors at midfield before the game that his team was going to kick Tennessee's ass. They did, too, winning 21-10. Well, unfortunately, my pep talk didn't work. The team played hard, but Tennessee won, 16-7, meaning that I retired with an 0-1 record in pep talks.

At halftime, in honor of the fact that I had agreed to allow the university to use my likeness in order to raise some money, C.M. presented me with a framed print and I got a nice ovation from the Commonwealth Stadium crowd. That evening, I was feeling pretty good, all things considered, until Channel 27 came on with a tape of my pregame talk to the team. It had been my understanding that the tape wouldn't be used until the end of the year, as part of a video of my final season, and that it would be edited. I had used the word "ass" four times in the talk, which is something I would never do in public, and doggone if they didn't run the whole thing. I was pretty upset about it. I got a warm letter of apology from Ralph Gabbard, the head of WKYT-TV, who assured me that the response to the piece had been absolutely positive and that the station had not had one negative call. I guess I got too uptight about it to begin with.

Although I was disappointed with the final 3-8 record, I reminded myself of how much more time it takes to build a winner in football because of the numbers involved. I really like Bill Curry and have a lot of confidence that he's going to get the job done. He's a class act, and he can rest assured that nobody's going to be rooting for him harder than me.

Moving into basketball season, I frankly didn't see how the Cats were going to top their 22-6 record of the previous year. When I looked at the team, I still saw only one player, Jamal Mashburn, who was a cinch to make it in the NBA. And besides the fact that Alabama figured to be tough as usual and that LSU still had Shaquille O'Neal, you had Arkansas coming into the league with a veteran team that had Final Four potential. But Pitino didn't seem as worried about the talent as he did about a lack of senior leadership — which, in restrospect, seems funny. But I remember him telling me, "I'm afraid that while everybody else is dancing, our players will be standing in the back of the room." That reminded me of what Coach Rupp had said before the 1957-58 season about the team that came to be known as the "Fiddlin' Five."

The season opened with the Preseason NIT and a lot of talk about Rick taking his team back to New York's Madison Square Garden to play Eddie Sutton and Oklahoma State in the semifinals. But the Cats, after opening with an impressive win at home against West Virginia, ruined the scenario by losing a shocker to Pittsburgh, 85-67, also in Rupp. That was not the only game that Kentucky lost, but I believe it was the only game where the team went into a game supremely overconfident.

Dick Vitale was in town to telecast the games and he told anyone who would listen what a mismatch it was and that Kentucky would trounce the Panthers. I think the players heard him and, unfortunately, believed him. Relying almost totally on the three-pointer, they were a horrible seven-of-36 from that range. Everybody was sort of upset at that point. But, looking back, that loss to Pitt may have been a blessing in disguise. That gave Pitino 11 or 12 days to work with the players before the next game. He worked them hard, but he also made them understand that they were the kind of team that had to leave it all on the floor every time to be any good.

Since we already had our hotel reservations and plane tickets, Frances and I, along with Ralph Hacker, his dad Joe and Sally Crutcher, decided to go ahead and make the New York trip. When I told Rick, he did a very nice thing for us. "I'm going to give you an early Christmas present," he said. He took care of dinner for us one night at Bravo Gianni's, the New York restaurant that his Lexington restaurant is modeled after, and he got us tickets to "Phantom of the Opera." On the fourth row! I tell you, it was terrific. Frances and I just had a great time, thanks to Rick.

When the team returned to action on December 4, it was against Massachusetts, Pitino's alma mater. Before the season, when people looked at the game and snickered, Rick told them that UMass was going to have a really good team. He was right, too. Although Kentucky won the game, 92-69, that was a bit misleading. The visitors had just won the Great Alaska Shootout and they were dead-tired from that long trip back. The most energetic one of the bunch was the coach, John Calipari, whose clothes and sideline behavior were so much like Rick's that it was almost comical.

The Cats then went to Indianapolis to play IU in what was left of the Big Four Classic. The four-year-old double-header, which had also included Louisville and Notre Dame, fell apart when ABC stipulated it would only be interested in televising the double-header if they would move the date of the game. The teams refused. Then, CBS entered the picture, but wanted only the UK-IU game. The Big Four Classic became the Big Two Classic. Even so, the Hoosier Dome crowd of 34,704 was only slightly smaller than the double-header used to draw, which tells you a lot about the fan appeal of both UK and IU.

From my standpoint, this is when the farewell gifts started. Just before tipoff, I was surprised when I looked up and saw Bobby Knight coming across the floor toward me with something under his arm. He grabbed me by the arm and said, on the air, that he really appreciated the friendship we'd had over the years and that he wanted to give me a little something to remember him by. Then he gave me one of those red Indiana sweaters that have become his trademark. I really appreciated it because I'd always admired him so much. But somehow I think I'll be better off in Kentucky if I wear that sweater only in the privacy of my home.

The game turned out to be an early season classic, with UK holding on for a 76-74 win when IU's Greg Graham missed a three-pointer just before the final horn. Although Deron Feldhaus gave the Cats a big spark off the bench, the happiest UK player was Sean Woods, who was from Indianapolis and had a lot of relatives at the game.

The next game, an 82-36 mismatch against Southwest Texas State on December 10, is memorable only because of Pitino's post-game show, in which he ripped Channel 27 for airing a report that he was thinking about taking the head coaching job with the New Jersey Nets. He had already denied that report repeatedly, and was frustrated that the media in Kentucky seemed to refuse to believe him. As that furor finally began to die down, Kentucky beat Morehead State, 101-84, and then blistered an Arizona State team that had been highly regarded before the season, 94-68. The Arizona State game was the one in which Dale Brown, who had come to UK advertised as a three-point specialist, finally lived up to his reputation, connecting for six consecutive threes on his way to a 24-point night.

If the Pitt game was gut-check No. 1 in the season, No. 2 came against Georgia Tech on December 21 in the Kuppenheimer Classic. Down 20 points and with Pitino in the locker room, having been ejected for getting two technical fouls, the Cats mounted a furious comeback that eventually fell a point short, 81-80. Although that dropped the team's record to 6-2, it was a good indication of the sort of character that was to become the team's trademark.

After a workmanlike 73-63 win over Ohio University in Cincinnati's Riverfront Coliseum on December 23, the Cats returned home to play Louisville on Saturday, December 28. The day before the game, I stopped off at Louisville's practice to say hello to Denny Crum. The Cardinals had just beaten LSU in Baton Rouge on a last-second shot by freshman Keith LeGree, and Denny told me that had been the first time in his 21 seasons at Louisville that his team had won a game on the last shot. That amazed me, but I wasn't about to argue with Denny's memory, which is about as sharp as his coaching ability. Before the game, I remarked that I thought the IU rivalry had grown to be more emotional for UK fans than the one with Louisville, but I was ready to take that back after UK's 103-89 win before 24,295 hungry fans in Rupp Arena. I suppose the thing that has surprised me the most about the UK-U of L series is the way the Cats have dominated it. The win gave them a 6-3 edge in the regular-season games.

The Louisville game was victory No. 2 in a winning streak that would reach eight games, giving the Cats a 14-2 record heading into their game against Tennessee on January 21 in Knoxville. This one was close most of the way, with Tennessee's Allan Houston and UK's Mashburn both showing their All-American credentials, but the Vols blew it open in the final minutes for a 107-85 win. I thought it was the worst officiated game of the season, on both sides. The Cats were whistled for 41 fouls, which led to an astounding 59 free-throw attempts by Tennessee. If every game was called like that one, basketball wouldn't be nearly the popular game it is.

Next up, on January 25, was the first Rupp Arena appearance by Arkansas and its terrific senior trio of Todd Day, Oliver Miller and Lee Mayberry. The fans had been looking forward to the game for so long that the atmosphere was electric. Usually it only gets that way when Tennessee or LSU is in town, but Arkansas came into the league with such a big reputation that it automatically became a special game for everybody.

Although Mashburn got into early foul trouble, committing three in a two-minute span, the Cats played the more talented Razorbacks pretty even until late in the game, when coach Nolan Richardson's team pulled away from a 78-77 lead with 8:07 remaining for a 105-88 win. The Cats missed Mashburn, who only had four points in 18 minutes, and they never could come up with an answer for the beefy Miller's long run-out passes to Day, Mayberry and others. I was so impressed with the way Arkansas handled the hostile environment that I saw 'em as a legitimate Final Four team.

After a 96-78 win over Ole Miss on January 29 at home, the Cats traveled to Baton Rouge for a Sunday, February 2, afternoon date with LSU. Although they did a commendable job against the incredible hulk of O'Neal — if you can say holding him to 20 points and 20 rebounds is commendable — the Cats did themselves in with some frigid shooting, especially from three-point land. Hitting only eight of 44 from beyond the arc, UK shot a miserable 27.5 percent for the game on the way to a 74-53 drubbing. I thought Rick's game plan was sound, considering the formidable presence of O'Neal in the paint, but he second-guessed himself for not insisting that they take it inside more. I think this is when he realized that the team needed more of an inside game to balance the three-point shooting because from there on, UK did a much better job of getting the ball inside.

With three double-digit losses in their last four games, the Cats found themselves at gut-check No. 3. I think a lot of fans were really worried at this point that the whole thing was getting way from the team, that maybe they had been overrated. But Pitino never wavered. He kept insisting that there was nothing to get panicky about and, as usual, he proved to be right.

Regrouping themselves, the Cats won eight of their final nine in the regular season, losing only to Florida, 79-62, in

Gainesville. Probably the biggest confidence-builder during that stretch was a 107-83 win over a strong Alabama team on February 12 in Rupp Arena. That was only the second time that anybody had gone over 100 points against one of Wimp Sanderson's teams. The first came when Pitino's 1987 Providence team thumped a great Alabama team, 103-82, in the NCAA Mideast Regional on its way to the Final Four. Maybe it's time for Wimp to turn the tables on Rick and begin wearing Armani suits whenever he plays one of Pitino's teams. After all, if Rick can wear plaid when he's coaching against Wimp, turn-about is fair play.

The final home win, 99-88 over Tennessee on Saturday, March 7, is one I'll never forget. Since it was to be my last UK game in Rupp Arena, somebody came up with the idea of having me burst through a paper hoop before the game, just as the seniors always do. But I squashed that because I felt it would detract from the seniors and, my, I wanted more than anybody for Feldhaus, Pelphrey, Farmer and Woods to get all the attention and credit they so richly deserved. So then the UK folks came up with the idea of doing something for me after the game. That was fine, but, as I told Rick, "For goodness sake, don't get beat because then nobody will stay."

My last UK game in Rupp. It really hit me hard the night before the game. I was so nervous and melancholy that I'll bet I didn't sleep more than two hours. The morning of the game, I went down to tape Rick's show. On the way back home, I stopped to get some gas at one of those self-pump stations. As I was pumping, a young man who must have been in his late 20s came over to me and said, "God bless you." That's all. That really got to me.

It was a great afternoon for the seniors. The crowd really tore the place down when each was introduced, as well it should have, because I don't think the basketball program has ever had four more special seniors. The only thing that kept me going through the broadcast was that I might be back in Rupp doing the Southeast Regional for the CBS Network (which didn't happen, as it turned out). But everything turned out well. The team played really well and won the game. And just about everybody stayed, even though we had 10 or 12 minutes of broadcasting before they got to the ceremony for me.

Well, it was just tremendous. They played some tapes highlighting various points of my career, and C.M. presented both Frances and me with a lifetime press pass to all UK athletics contests. But the part that got to me the most was when Richie Farmer spoke for the team. He said that I'd been his hero before he had come to UK. "Now that I've got to know you, you're still my hero and I love you," he said.

Boy, that tore my guts out. I had made a deal with C.M. going into it that I would say something only if I felt like it. After what Richie said, it took me a few moments to pull myself together. I didn't say much. Just thank you and how much I appreciated the support and God bless 'em. I was lucky to get through that without crying, and I know it's going to be a long time before I can look at the tape without tearing up.

Getting ready for the SEC Tournament in Birmingham, Pitino said that, physically, he didn't think the Cats could press for three straight days. Well, he lied like a dog. They pressed everything in sight from beginning to end. In the first game against Vanderbilt, which had advanced by eliminating Ole Miss, Rick got so mad at Mashburn for not shooting more often that he yanked him out for a good butt-chewing. It must have done some good, because Mashburn went to war, scoring 24 points and grabbing 10 rebounds in UK's 76-57 win, and he stayed at war for the rest of the post-season.

That set up a rematch with LSU in the semifinals. Well, sort of a rematch. The Tigers had to play without O'Neal, who had been ejected from their win over Tennessee for getting into an altercation with Carlus Groves. It wouldn't have been any big deal except for LSU coach Dale Brown, who came on the floor after the players had been separated and began shoving Groves. The officials didn't handle it very well. If anything, Dale should have been kept out of the next game instead of Shaquille. Going into the game, Rick warned the players that LSU would fight even harder without its superstar. He was right, as usual, and the Cats had to work hard for their 80-74 victory, although not nearly as hard as Alabama had to work to upset Arkansas in a semifinal that was the most spectacular game of the tournament.

Although Wimp's team was really tired heading into the championship game on March 15 — as tired as I've ever seen a team — they hung tough in a helluva first half that saw nine lead changes. But Kentucky, which trailed, 32-29, at the break, really wore 'em out in the second half. After UK's 80-54 victory in its first SEC Tournament since 1989, Mashburn, who had 28 points and 13 rebounds against Alabama, was named the MVP. Pelphrey also made the all-tournament team. It was during the tournament that Mashburn had joined Rex Chapman as the only UK players to surpass 1,000 career points while still a sophomore. He also passed Rex to become the highest-scoring soph in UK history.

There's nothing like being with a team just after it's won a championship. After the win over Alabama, we got on the bus and went to a restaurant called O'Charley's, where UK had arranged to have a private dining room with a TV so everybody could watch the NCAA Tournament pairings show from Kansas City. Before the show, Rick told the team he thought it would be either the No. 1 seed in the West or the No. 2 seed in the East. When it was announced that UK would be the No. 2 seed in the East and would open its NCAA play against Old Dominion in Worcester, Mass., Rick told them to pronounce it *Wuss-ter* instead of *Wer-ches-ter*. Everybody laughed. For the four seniors, their first NCAA Tournament appearance finally was a reality.

After the SEC Tournament, Dan Issel, who does a pretty

darned good job as a TV color man, told me he thought my
goodbye at Rupp Arena had been one of the most amazing
things he had ever seen. "All those people staying that
long," Dan said. But he also had a sobering thought for me:
"Now every UK game might be your last one." He was right
because that's how life goes in the NCAA Tournament.

Once we got to Worcester, which is only about 45 minutes from Providence, where Rick used to coach, Pitino
organized a trip to Providence, where we were met by a
group of his friends. Then we all went to Camille's, which
he thinks is the greatest Italian restaurant in the world. We
had a fun group: John Marinatto, the Providence AD; Billy
Reynolds, the Providence sportswriter who had worked with
Rick on his first book; Dick "Hoops" Weiss, the
Philadelphia writer who was doing a book on the season
with Rick; Ken "Jersey Red" Ford, an old friend of Rick's;
Tom Wallace, editor of *Cawood on Kentucky*; and some others. When the waitress came to take my order, I pointed to
Rick and said, "I'll have whatever he has."

He ordered some appetizers for all of us, which included
something I had never had before — fried squid, also known
as calamari. Well, I got a little confused. A lot of the talk
that night was about UMass, which UK had the chance of
meeting again in the East Regional semifinals. As we were
leaving, I asked Rick, "What was that stuff we ate? That
fried Calipari?" I meant the squid, not the UMass coach, but
Rick thought it was so funny he told Bill Raftery, who men-

tioned it on CBS.

Under NCAA rules, a team is required to hold a public practice at the game site, but most coaches also have private practices elsewhere so they can work on their game plan. The public practices are mostly just shooting exhibitions. The day before the Old Dominion game, Rick held the private practice at Holy Cross. He told the players about Bob Cousy and Tom Heinsohn, both of whom had played there. Then he went to work on the game plan for Old Dominion.

All week he had said that he was shocked that a No. 15 seed could be that good. He wasn't just kidding, either. In fact, when we taped the pre-game show at 11 a.m. on game day, Rick was the most nervous I had ever seen him in the three years I had known him. He was tight as a banjo string, and for good reason. The Cats shot only 33 percent in the first half and had only a two-point lead. They finally won, 88-69, but only because of a gut-it-out, blue-collar effort on defense. After the game, Rick told me on the post-game show that it was the most nervous he had been as a coach. I guess, after the team had come so far, he didn't want to see them ambushed right off the bat.

The win over Old Dominion moved UK to a second-round game against Iowa State, which had beaten UNC-Charlotte in its opening game. This time both teams shot the lights out. The seniors really came through, each one of them scoring in double figures, but Iowa State fought for its life before finally falling, 106-98, and opening the way for the Cats to play UMass and Coach Calamari — ah, Calipari — in the East Regional semifinals in Philadelphia. The way I looked at it, advancing to the Sweet 16 removed any and all pressure. The team's 28-6 record was far better than anybody had a right to expect. Anything that happened the rest of the way was strictly icing on the cake.

Before the UMass rematch, Pitino, once again adopting his role as professor of hoops history, held the team's private practice in the Palestra. I'd done games there years ago, back when, along with Madison Square Garden in New York and the Boston Garden, it was one of the most famous arenas in the East. The so-called Big Five — Penn, La Salle, Villanova, St. Joseph's and Temple — all used to play their home games there. But then they began building their own campus arenas and the Spectrum was built for the 76ers, relegating the Palestra to fossil status.

The thing I remember most about the practice at the Palestra is that Rick got on John Pelphrey like you wouldn't believe. I think he often used John to get across a message to everybody because he knew John could take the criticism whereas others were too sensitive.

Knowing that this UMass team would be a lot more rested and better prepared than the one they had whipped in December, the Cats came out and really went to war, building a 20-point lead with five minutes still left in the first half. But Calipari's team cut it to eight on a 70-footer to end the first half and had gotten it down to four in the second period when, suddenly, Calipari was hit with a technical, apparently for being out of the coach's box. Everybody thought that was rather strange, considering how hyper both Calipari and Pitino are on the sidelines, and it definitely took the starch out of the Minutemen. I don't think it cost them the game, but the final score might have been closer than the final 87-77 by which the Cats won and advanced to the East final against Duke, the 31-2 team that had been ranked No. 1 from day one.

Most of the national commentators, especially Mike Francesa and Digger Phelps on CBS, gave UK absolutely no chance, which, by the way, begs these questions: Just where did CBS dig up Francesa? And considering Digger's track record in NCAA play, what does he know about what it takes to win after the first round? Anyway, I thought Richie Farmer put it best when he said, the day before the game, "We respect 'em, but we don't fear 'em."

Nobody, of course, expected one of the greatest college games ever played, but that's exactly what they got. UK led by as much as eight in the first half, only to let Duke take a five-point lead, 50-45, at the break. In the second half, led by 6'11" Player-of-the-Year Christian Laettner, the Blue Devils kicked it out to 12 and seemed ready to close it out. But here came the Cats, clawing and scratching until they finally tied it at 87-87 on Dale Brown's three-pointer.

Duke's frustration was most evident when Laettner put his foot in the stomach of UK freshman Aminu Timberlake, who was lying helpless on the floor. The officials rightly tagged him for a technical,which was the last thing Duke needed at that point. By then it was anybody's game, and it ended in a 93-93 tie, sending it into overtime. I thought UK had just worn Duke out with its relentless pressure, while also confusing the Blue Devils with the zone defense Pitino put in especially for the game, a move that turned out to be a real coaching gem. On the other hand, however, UK was in serious foul trouble.

Trailing 102-101 and with Mashburn having fouled out, UK came out of a timeout and seemed to get the game-winning basket when Woods made an incredible shot — almost a Hail Mary — over Laettner that kissed off the glass and swished through. When the Blue Devils called time with only 2.1 seconds showing on the clock, my partner, Ralph Hacker, began talking about how Kentucky had this one wrapped up. I had to break in and remind Ralph that you could never take anything for granted against a team like Duke. Sure enough, when play resumed, Duke's Grant Hill fired a perfect 75-foot pass to Laettner, who faked right, spun left, and shot a 17-footer that hit nothing but net. Duke 104, UK 103. As the ball went through I shouted, "It's good...and that's why Duke is number one."

Everybody on the UK side was stunned. I felt like a train had run over me. A Boston sportswriter named Bob Ryan, who was sitting in front of me, turned around and held up a sheet of paper on which he had written, "Greatest game ever?" I would have agreed if that last shot had missed.

A few moments later, as I was into my goodbye comments on the post-game show, I was surprised to see Duke coach Mike Krzyzewski standing there and wanting to put a headset on. Talk about a class act! He told the UK fans that they should be proud of their team because this was the greatest game he had ever been a part of. Then he congratulated me for a great career, thanked me for what I had done for college basketball and wished me well. Even though I was pretty numb at the time, I really appreciated that.

When I got back home, Frances kind of put it in perspective for me, as she always does. She pointed out that if you have to get beat, at least let 'em carry you out on your shield. The team had given its last full measure and who could ask for anything more? I thought that hit the nail right on the head. Oh, I know there was a lot of second-guessing about whether Pelphrey or Feldhaus should have been going for the ball on that pass to Laettner instead of being behind him. But, heck, I say let's just give Laettner credit for making a great play. I like what *Herald-Leader* columnist Chuck Culpepper wrote after the Final Four. He ranked Duke No. 1, Kentucky No. 2 and nobody else higher than No. 5. That's about the way I felt, too. Remembering what Pitino had told me before the season, it made me happy to know that Kentucky's kids had turned out to be dancers, not wallflowers. Kentucky was Kentucky again, and that made me feel tremendous.

The next week I went on to Minneapolis to do my last Final Four for the CBS Radio Network. On Friday, the CBS television people came to me and asked my permission to cut into my broadcast sometime during the championship game. I said, "No problem," then forgot all about it. I didn't know until after the championship game, in which Duke beat Michigan, 71-51, to get its second title in a row, that they had done it. I appreciated it, but, otherwise, I didn't feel much emotion about taking off the headset and microphone for the last time. Oh, it dawned on me and I thought about it. But it certainly wasn't as bad as realizing that when Laettner's shot went in, that was my last UK game.

On the way back from Minneapolis, C.M. Newton told me that at the honors celebration on Tuesday, April 7, he was going to make the surprise announcement that a jersey would be retired in honor of each of the four seniors. I told him I thought it was one of the great ideas of all-time. Those four guys didn't put up the numbers that UK's All-Americans did, but I can't think of four players who meant more to Kentucky basketball. I think everybody agrees, because when C.M. made the announcement, the crowd of about 10,000 really went wild. The seniors were shocked. It was just a great outpouring of love.

A week or so later, I had an opportunity to know just how those four seniors felt. A tribute dinner was held for me in Rupp Arena, with the proceeds going to endow a scholarship for UK athletes who want to come back to school and finish work on their degrees. It turned out to be a wonderful evening for Frances and me. Many old and dear friends were on hand to say hello, along with past and present UK coaches and players.

Believe me, when that night was over, Frances and I knew what being loved and appreciated really meant.

In a way, I guess, that tribute dinner kind of served to bring to an end my final year, which just seemed to fly by in a big hurry. It's been an eventful and busy year. Most of all, though, it's been a very emotional year. It's just not easy to stop doing something you genuinely love.

But what a year it was! Thanks to what Rick and his Wildcats were able to achieve, I couldn't have asked for a better year to step down. I'm going out with the Wildcats back on top, where they rightfully belong.

Come to think of it, my first season — 1953-54 — with the football Cats' 7-2-1 record and the roundball Cats' 25-0 record, and my last season — 1991-92 — with Rick's club finishing at 29-7 are somehow symbolic to me.

They're the perfect bookends for what has been a wonderful and exciting career.

Appendix

Cawood's Lists

In his 42 years at Kentucky, Adolph Rupp steudfastly refused to name his top player or players. He reasoned that doing so would serve only to make a few of his players happy and most of them mad. Coach Rupp was probably wise to refrain from such an endeavor, but I never claimed to be as smart as "The Baron." So, here are a few lists that I've come up with during my 39 years of broadcasting sports.

TOP 10 UK BASKETBALL PLAYERS

In the order of which they played during my 39 years broadcasting.

• **CLIFF HAGAN**. He was a shy, introverted young man while he was at Kentucky until he stepped across the white lines. Then Cliff became a tiger with supreme confidence and magnificent skills. He was one of the most graceful players I ever saw, and he had the ability to destroy an opponent with his hook shots inside or go out to the wing and rip a defense apart.

• **FRANK RAMSEY**. Frank was a teammate of Cliff's on the 1953-54 team that posted a perfect 25-0 record. At 6'3", Frank was only an inch shorter than Hagan, but they were as different as two players could be. Frank was a slasher going to the basket, but if the defense sagged off he could bury his shot from long range. He was a defensive stopper and just a great all-around player.

• **COTTON NASH**. He was named to the All-American team every year he played for the Wildcats. Cotton, at 6'5", was small for a center, but he was like a cat down in the paint. He could also take an opponent out on the court and glide past him. Cotton was just a magnificent athlete. He was also one of the most important players in UK's history. Cotton literally carried the program — on the court and at the box office — on his back during a time when UK didn't have its usual amount of talent. I can't say enough about Cotton Nash.

• **LOUIE DAMPIER**. If I were to pick the best outside shooter who ever wore the blue and white, Louie would get my vote. Dampier could bust a zone wide open. He was such an excellent shooter that his other skills were often overlooked. Louie was a solid defensive player and, like most great players, he wanted the ball when the game was on the line. Louie was small but he had great tenacity and courage.

• **DAN ISSEL**. He is the leading scorer in UK's storied history. Dan had a lot of pride and intelligence, and the bigger the challenge, the better he played. He was only a 6'9" center but like most of Kentucky's best pivotmen, he could take a taller opponent out on the court and put it to him. Roy Skinner, who coached at Vanderbilt, said Issel improved more from each year to the next than any player he ever saw. Dan had a great work ethic to go with his great talent.

• **KEVIN GREVEY**. He was one of several outstanding left-handers to play for UK. Kevin had a great touch on the ball from the outside and could also take it to the hoop. He had a little bit of a tendency to shoot in streaks, but when he got it on a roll he could light up the scoreboard.

Kevin had the ability to just take over a game. Kevin was the best player on a very good 1975 basketball team.

• **JACK GIVENS**. He already had the nickname "Goose" when he came to UK from Bryan Station High School in Lexington. While at Kentucky, Jack also picked up the name "Silk" and that really described just how smooth he was on the court. Jack was also a gifted left-hander and is the third highest scorer in UK history. He saved his best for last, and his 41-point outing against Duke in the 1978 NCAA final was one of the most awesome offensive performances of any Kentucky player I ever saw.

• **KYLE MACY**. Like most sons of basketball coaches, Kyle knew the game well. He was highly intelligent and ran the team like a coach. Kyle could get the ball to a teammate for a good shot or he could take the shot and hit it himself. Kyle was one of the best clutch players to ever play at UK. I don't know of any player I would choose ahead of him to take the last shot or go to the free throw line with the game on the line.

• **SAM BOWIE**. When Sam came to UK as a freshman, I boldly predicted he would be the best player UK ever had. He may have been, but he was plagued with serious injuries his entire career. A true seven-footer who could run the floor like a gazelle, Bowie was also a fine defensive player. He once blocked nine shots in a game. After being named to the All-American team following his sophomore season, the injury jinx hit and Sam didn't play again for two years. He came back for his senior season to lead the Cats to the Final Four.

• **KENNY WALKER**. They called him "Sky" and if ever a name fit a player, that one did. Kenny could really jump. Occasionally he would take part in dunking the basketball with the other players after practice and when he did, he was so good at it that the other players stood and marveled. Kenny is the second-leading scorer at Kentucky, but he could do it all. He was twice named to the All-American team and was just an outstanding player.

Among those outstanding players I left out were **Vernon Hatton, Johnny Cox, Larry Pursiful, Pat Riley, Larry Conley, Mike Casey, Jimmy Dan Conner, Rick Robey, Ed Davender and Rex Chapman.**

Come to think of it, that's a pretty formidable list. Now I know why Coach Rupp hesitated to pick his top 10.

UNSUNG HEROES

*There have been many great basketball players at Kentucky through-
out my 39 years who did not make All-American but who were vital to the
success of the program. This would be my top 10 underrated players.*

• **LOU TSIOROPOULOS**. He was a member of the Big Three on the
undefeated 1953-54 team with Cliff Hagan and Frank Ramsey. Lou could
score, he averaged in double figures — but he was overshadowed by
Hagan and Ramsey. Lou did the dirty work. He rebounded and he always
took the opponent's best inside player to defend. He was a tremendous
defensive player.

• **ADRIAN SMITH**. He came out of the junior college ranks to join
the "Fiddlin' Five" at Kentucky in the late '50s and was an important cog
in winning the NCAA championship in 1958. Vernon Hatton told me one
time that once "Odie" joined up with a bunch of old veterans at UK, they
decided to make him a passer. He was good at it but he could also stroke
it from outside too.

• **LARRY PURSIFUL**. One game day, as the team was leaving the
hotel to practice, Coach Rupp said, "Larry, you might as well stay here.
You won't shoot in the game anyway." What Coach Rupp wanted was for
Larry to shoot more often. Larry could not only shoot well, he could play
the game of basketball. After UK lost to a great Ohio State team in 1962,
Buckeye coach Fred Taylor said to me, "We knew about Nash, but where
did you get Pursiful? He's the best guard we've played all season."

• **LARRY CONLEY**. I think he could have been All-SEC without
question if he hadn't decided to relinquish his scoring for the good of that
1966 Rupp's Runts team. Larry could play defense and for his size he was
an excellent rebounder. But what Larry Conley provided in leadership
can't be counted in statistics. I think he is the best passer to ever play at
UK in my time.

• **TOMMY KRON**. He gave up scoring, as did Conley, to help that
1966 team become an outstanding ballclub. At 6'5", Tommy played guard
and was the tallest member of the team. He was an excellent floor general
and a tenacious defensive player. That team played the 1-3-1 zone better
than any team I've ever seen and the biggest reason was the play of Kron
at the point.

• **JIMMY DAN CONNER**. Tough as hickory. He was always at his best in the big games. His play against North Carolina in 1974 engineered the most important win in a season that culminated with the Wildcats finishing as national runners-up. When I once said over the air that Jimmy Dan had taken a bad shot in a game, he took me out on the practice floor to the same spot a few days later and made six in a row.

• **LARRY JOHNSON**. If Larry had been a better shooter, he would have been an All-American because he had everything else going for him. He could fly. He was so quick, he could strip the ball right out of the hands of a dribbler. He played his heart out every time he stepped on the court. Larry was a very unselfish player who was always looking to get the ball to an open teammate.

• **ED DAVENDER**. He wasn't a flashy player and he never got the recognition I thought he deserved. Ed is the only Kentucky player to score over 1,500 points and hand out over 400 assists. As good as he was on offense, he was even better on defense. Ed was a stopper. He could take the other team's best guard and just shut him down. He was one of those players who just got better and better as his career went along.

• **REGGIE HANSON**. He would make everyone's All-Smile team, but Reggie could also play basketball. Reggie was a frail looking 6'7" but he was a very strong person. Reggie gave the team tremendous leadership and he could carry the load at either end of the floor. He was very mobile down in the paint and could hold his own defensively against much bigger centers. Reggie could have transferred without sanctions, after the NCAA penalties, but he decided to stay. No player had a bigger impact on leading Kentucky from the rubble back to prominence.

SIXTH MEN

During my 39 years, UK has had a host of excellent players who were super subs, or as it has lately become more popularly known — the "sixth man." These are players, many of whom started at one stage of their career, who could come off the bench and provide an instant lift for the Wildcats. Here are my top five Wildcat super subs in the order in which they played.

• **DON MILLS**. The 6'7" Mills, a Berea native, started his final two seasons at UK, but was a valuable sixth man on the 1958 NCAA champion Fiddlin' Five bunch. Mills was superb in the 1958 title game, coming off the bench to score nine points in the 84-72 win over Seattle.

• **JAMES LEE**. This 6'5" Lexington native was probably the quintessential sixth man because he not only spurred on the team, he also spurred on the crowd with those left-handed monstrous dunks that rattled the rafters. Lee was also an excellent defensive player, but it was for his signature dunks, like the one that ended the 1978 championship game against Duke, that he is best remembered.

• **JAY SHIDLER**. Shidler, like the next two guys coming up, was a starter almost as much as he was a sub. Still, it was his long-range bombing that made this blonde-haired Indiana native a true crowd favorite. When he was on, he could light up a scoreboard faster than a Wall Street inside trader can line up crooked deals. Oh, how he would have loved the three-point shot.

• **DERON FELDHAUS**. For my money, Feldhaus is, without question, one of the two best sixth men in UK history. Lee is the other. When Feldhaus entered a game, he brought many things to the team...scoring ability, hustle, defense, guts and hard-nosed courage. Sixth man or not, Feldhaus was usually on the floor when the game was on the line.

• **RICHIE FARMER**. Although Farmer moved into the starting lineup on a permanent basis late in his senior year, he was, for the most part, an outstanding player off the bench. Farmer was instant offense when he came in and, like Shidler, he could wake up a quiet and lethargic crowd. Farmer was also a superb clutch player, one of those guys you want taking the last shot or shooting the last free throw.

SEC ALL-OPPONENT TEAM
In chronological order

1. Bob Pettit, LSU
2. Bailey Howell, Mississippi State
3. Clyde Lee, Vanderbilt
4. Pete Maravich, LSU
5. Leon Douglas, Alabama
6. Bernard King, Tennessee
7. Ernie Grunfeld, Tennessee
8. Dominique Wilkins, Georgia
9. Charles Barkley, Auburn
10. Shaquille O'Neal, LSU

ALL-OPPONENT TEAM
In chronological order

1. Tom Gola, La Salle
2. Jerry West, West Virginia
3. Guy Rodgers, Temple
4. Elgin Baylor, Seattle
5. Jerry Lucas, Ohio State
6. Austin Carr, Notre Dame
7. Jim McDaniels, Western Kentucky
8. Kent Benson, Indiana
9. Rodney McCray, Louisville
10. David Robinson, Navy

TOP OPPOSING COACHES

1. Whack Hyder, Georgia Tech
2. Babe McCarthy, Mississippi State
3. Ray Mears, Tennessee
4. Bob Knight, Indiana
5. Joel Evans, Auburn

BEST UK FOOTBALL PLAYERS

In my 39 years broadcasting football, I could count on one hand the top teams that have represented UK. But there have been many outstanding players who have come through the program during that time. Here are the ones I would choose as the best.

OFFENSE

ENDS: STEVE MEILINGER, RICK KESTNER

Meilinger, as I've said before, was just a tremendous athlete. I sincerely believe Steve could have played any position on the team and done it well. While he played several positions at UK, end was his best. There has never been anybody who played it better at Kentucky.

Kestner was big and had good speed for a receiver, but I think Rick's biggest asset was a great set of hands. I don't believe in the three years he played at Kentucky I ever saw him drop a pass. He could catch the football in the open field or in a crowd.

TACKLES: SAM BALL, WARREN BRYANT

Both had good size and strength and both were excellent blockers for ball carriers or protecting the passer. Ball had a great mentality for the game of football. He was supremely confident of his ability and provided strong leadership to his teammates. Warren had a quieter nature, but he also provided great leadership by his play on the field. Both were outstanding football players at UK.

GUARDS: RAY CORRELL, DERMONTTI DAWSON

They both had one thing in common that is rare for an offensive lineman — they both could really run. Correll played on that 1953 team during my first season at UK. I believe he could go downfield covering a punt better than any player in my time. He got there fast and he got there in a bad mood. Dawson also had that rare gift for an offensive lineman; he had superb speed for a man his size. When he blocked for an end sweep, he was fast enough to get to the corner well ahead of the ball carrier.

CENTER: IRV GOODE

He was a great technician. Goode always graded out high when the coach viewed the film. He seldom made a mental mistake and was an excellent blocker. It was no big surprise when Goode was named to the 1961 All-American team.

QUARTERBACK: RICK NORTON–DERRICK RAMSEY

This is the only position on the team that I couldn't separate, so I made it a tie. Norton was the prototype quarterback while Ramsey was just a great athlete who could have made the starting team at several positions. Norton had the best touch on a long pass of any quarterback in my time. He could hit an opponent with a game-breaker in a split second. Ramsey was just the opposite. He could connect on the short pass, but his real forte was running the football. He was big and strong and just a great athlete. He was instrumental in Kentucky's 10-1 record in 1977, the best UK team in my time.

RUNNING BACKS: RODGER BIRD, SONNY COLLINS, MARK HIGGS.

None had blazing speed, but all three had an important key to being a top running back: All three were explosive. All three would be at full speed after just a few yards. Bird was a very gifted athlete out of Corbin, Ky. He was the best of the three at improvising. If he found his path blocked on an end sweep, he had the uncanny ability to reverse his field and often turn a bad play into a long gainer. Bird was also a good passer and some of his ad-lib aerials went for touchdowns.

Collins was a threat to go the distance every time he touched the football. When his line was able to get him into the secondary, he was a handful for opposing tacklers. Collins was just a superb athlete and a smooth-running tailback who would make any team a better team.

Higgs was the best broken-field runner of the three. I had a tendency to think of him as small, but even though he was only 5'7", he weighed close to 200 pounds and was strong as an ox. He could break tackles, but if he got into the open field, he wasn't going to be brought down by one tackler. I have seen him fake a defender so badly that the tackler wouldn't lay a finger on Higgs.

DEFENSE

ENDS: HOWARD SCHNELLENBERGER, ART STILL

Schnellenberger played in the days when players were required to play both offense and defense. He was what nowadays they call a blue-collar player. He had a great work ethic and went full bore both in practice and in the game. He was so consistent he made All-American in 1955 despite little support from the UK publicity office.

Still was one of the greatest athletes to ever suit up in a Kentucky uniform. He was big (6'7", 255 pounds) and he could run like a gazelle. He was so talented and so dominant that other teams tried to run away from his side of the line. He was at his best for the big games, and when Art Still was at his best, there has never been a better football player at Kentucky.

TACKLES: LOU MICHAELS, OLIVER BARNETT

Michaels could do it all. In addition to his great play at tackle, he punted, kicked off, kicked field goals and extra points. God did truly bless Michaels with great talent and great enthusiasm for the game of football. Even though he played on one of Kentucky's lesser teams, Michaels was the most-feared defensive lineman in the Southeastern Conference. He may have been responsible for bringing the "audible" to the SEC. The opposing quarterback would check where Michaels had lined up, then call the play to go the other way.

Barnett did not have the aggressive nature of Michaels. Off the field he was a very gentle person. He became much more aggressive as his career moved along, and by his senior year he was a real force on the defensive line. Barnett had tremendous quickness for a big guy and was certainly one of the best pass rushers to ever play for the Wildcats. UK coaches have been looking for another pass rushing tackle like Barnett ever since he graduated.

NOSE GUARD: RICHARD JAFFE

He played the position on Kentucky's best teams during the mid '70s and was one of many fine players at the spot Fran Curci developed. Jaffe wasn't exceptionally fast in the 40-yard dash, but he was very quick on the line of scrimmage and strong as Superman. He trained just as hard as he played and would be a winner on anybody's football team.

LINEBACKERS: JOE FEDERSPIEL, FRANK LeMASTER, JIM KOVACH

This talented trio had a lot in common. All three were big and fast and exceptionally hard hitters. All three were very intelligent. All of them were polite, softspoken people off the field who turned into monsters when they stepped across the white lines. Ironically, they followed each other at UK. When Federspiel moved to the NFL after the 1971 season, LeMaster was ready to take over. Kovach came right behind LeMaster. Kentucky has been blessed with a lot of outstanding linebackers, but I think I would go with that trio.

DEFENSIVE BACKS: DARRYL BISHOP, DALLAS OWENS, PAUL CALHOUN

Bishop and Owens had good size and good speed for their positions and both had a good nose for the ball. Both could turn interceptions into long gainers with their broken-field running. Bishop was a great tackler in the open field...maybe the best-ever at UK. Owens was so good in the defensive backfield that he could win a game for the Wildcats. Calhoun had nowhere near the speed of Bishop and Owens, but he had great anticipation for the football. His seven interceptions during the 1984 season rank second only to Jerry Claiborne.

SPECIALISTS

KICK RETURNS: DICKY LYONS

Despite playing on some of the weaker teams at UK, Lyons was a standout. He was good enough as an athlete to play several positions at UK, but he was an awesome punt and kickoff returner. He was the first player in the SEC to gain 1,000 yards returning punts and 1,000 yards returning kickoffs. It took Lyons a few steps to get rolling, but he had good speed and the most desire to go all the way of any player I ever saw.

PUNTING: PAUL CALHOUN

He is already a member of our all-time defensive backfield at UK, but Calhoun was the best punter in my 39 years. He averaged more than 42 yards a kick over his career and during his senior season his average was 44.61 yards per punt. He holds the UK record for the longest punt...80 yards. Calhoun was also the best at knowing when to punt and when to run from punt formation. His fourth-and-long gallop against Mississippi State set up the winning touchdown.

KICKER: DOUG PELFREY

He is the only member of the current UK team to make my All-Star list. Pelfrey was named to the All-SEC team last season. Kentucky has been blessed with some outstanding kickers, but Pelfrey holds the school's record for distance with two 53-yarders. But what sets Pelfrey apart is his performance under pressure. He beat Georgia two years ago with a field goal late in the game and defeated Cincinnati last season with a boot at the buzzer.

BEST SEC RESTAURANTS

For this list I polled my broadcasting partners over a lot of years, Ralph Hacker and Tom Devine, to help in coming up with our favorite eating places. In addition to our love of football and basketball, the three of us share a love for a great meal.

1. DREAMLAND, Tuscaloosa, Ala.
Ribs. That's it. Ribs. This shabby-looking restaurant serves barbecue ribs, white bread and a drink. Nothing else. But they are the best barbecue ribs you ever tasted.

2. RALPH AND CACOO'S, Baton Rouge, La.
There are a lot of excellent restaurants in Baton Rouge and some of them serve better dishes. But for seafood gumbo and hush puppies, nobody beats Ralph and Cacoo's.

3. THE YEARLING, Gainesville, Fla.
This place is located out in the boonies and we get lost every time we go. The speciality of the house is fried "cooter" which is alligator meat. The whole menu features outstanding food.

4. THE DAIRY BAR, Starkville, Miss.
This is located on the campus of Mississippi State University and serves the best milk shakes you ever tasted. They still make them the old-fashioned way with real ice cream, real milk and the whole works. It's a must stop on our tour of the SEC.

5. THE NASHVILLE HOUSE, Nashville, Ind.
Their specialty is fried biscuits and apple butter. But all of their food is good. I recommend their fried chicken and gravy. Whatever you order, don't forget the fried biscuits. Obviously, this restaurant is not in the SEC, but on your way to Bloomington, stop off. It's worth it.

FAVORITE KENTUCKY DERBIES
In chronological order

• **1948, CITATION.** This was before my broadcasting career began, but while I was at Centre College, I joined a fraternity brother for that Derby. I really liked Calumet Farm's Coaltown going into the race but the other Calumet color bearer was much the best. Citation was a great horse and went on to win the Triple Crown.

• **1961, CARRY BACK.** This was the first Derby I had the pleasure to broadcast and it was such a great race for Carry Back. He looked hopelessly beaten going down the back stretch, but he put on a tremendous rally and chased down Crozier in the stretch.

• **1964, NORTHERN DANCER.** If I were ranking the Derbys in order of favoritism instead of the years they were run, this one would probably head the list. Northern Dancer and Hill Rise locked up in a long and sustained drive to the wire with Northern Dancer winning by a neck. It was just a great, great horse race.

• **1973, SECRETARIAT.** My all-time favorite horse and the best I ever saw. He won the Derby and set the record that still stands. Secretariat ran each quarter of the Derby faster than the one before. An unbelievable performance. He went on to become the first Triple Crown winner in 25 years.

• **1984, SWALE.** I really liked that horse, but perhaps the most pleasing aspect of his win was to see the Claiborne Farm colors in the winner's circle. This great breeding farm had never won the race it most wanted to win. Swale did it for Claiborne.

Postscript

Signing Off

*D*oing this book has been a joyous and fulfilling experience for me. It's been fun to look back in the time vault and recall some of the people who have provided all of us sports fans with so many wonderful memories and so much pleasure.

It's been my great privilege and honor to serve as the link between the action on the fields of battle and you loyal fans who follow the Wildcats, Thoroughbred racing and all the other sports I've been fortunate to cover. I sincerely hope that by sharing some of these experiences with you, I have been able to bring you even closer to that great UK tradition we all cherish. Sure, there were a few memories that were painful, but most of them were exhilarating and thrilling.

I would be remiss if I didn't mention you fans, who are, without question, the greatest in the world. Your loyalty toward the UK program — and toward me — is almost mind-boggling. It's also greatly appreciated. Knowing that you were always there in my corner, that you were almost like an extended family to Frances and me, made doing this job that much more fun. You're the greatest.

Again, I would like to thank everyone who helped along the way, including those mentioned in this book and those who were unmentioned. Your great contributions have not gone unnoticed.

To end this book, I think it's somehow appropriate to borrow a line from a man I admired so much...Coach Rupp. During his final banquet, Coach Rupp ended with this thought, and I don't think he'd mind if I used it now.

I'd like to thank all those who traveled the glory road with me for these 39 years. It's been a memorable journey. This is Cawood Ledford, signing off, heading for home, and saying goodbye and God bless you all.